For Agnes,

Colin Bright

Angels Inspire a
Little Higher

Angels Inspire a Little Higher

Colum Wright

authorHOUSE®

AuthorHouse™
1663 Liberty Drive
Bloomington, IN 47403
www.authorhouse.com
Phone: 1-800-839-8640

Published by AuthorHouse   09/19/2012

ISBN: 978-1-4670-0160-1 (sc)
ISBN: 978-1-4772-3396-2 (e)

Any people depicted in stock imagery provided by Thinkstock are models, and such images are being used for illustrative purposes only.
Certain stock imagery © Thinkstock.

This book is printed on acid-free paper.

Because of the dynamic nature of the Internet, any web addresses or links contained in this book may have changed since publication and may no longer be valid. The views expressed in this work are solely those of the author and do not necessarily reflect the views of the publisher, and the publisher hereby disclaims any responsibility for them.

To my parents Kathleen and John.
My first teachers in the ways of faith.
Thank you.

I wish to acknowledge Eileen Havern, Anne Campbell R.I.P., John Campbell, Nicola Murphy, Louise Photography, Grace Rogan, Olivia Meara, Cora Brennan—Byrne, Doctor Marylou Murray, Anita Ryan, Father Vincent Sherlock, Marian McClory, Lily Byrne, Father Jack McArdle R.I.P., Father Liam Swords R.I.P., Sister Olive McConville, Mary McAleese, Gerard Trainor and all those who have taken the time down through the years to inspire me and pass on their favourite homilies, stories, poems and reflections.

The author and publishers acknowledge that certain amounts of the material in this publication were donated anonymously to Colum Wright who has to the best of his ability acknowledged the source of all other materials and published it with the permission of the owner where and however possible.

Reflection number 1

TRY TO BE AN ANGEL

A very young and successful executive was speeding down a side street in his new Jaguar without a thought for anyone or anything. All of a sudden a brick smashed into his Jag's side door. Angrily the driver slammed on his brakes and furiously reversed his Jag back to the spot where the brick had been thrown. Boiling over with rage he bounced out of his car, grabbed the nearest kid and pushed him up against the wall shouting at him, "What the hell was that all about and who are you? Just what the heck are you doing? That's a new car and that brick you threw is going to cost a lot of money. Why did you do it?"

The young boy was very apologetic. "Please, mister, stop, don't hurt me please, I'm sorry but I didn't know what else to do. I threw the brick because no one else would stop. I can't get anyone to help me." With tears dripping down his face and off his chin, the youth pointed to a spot beside a parked car. "It's my brother," he said. "He rolled off the kerb and fell out of his wheelchair. I can't lift him up." Sobbing, the boy asked the stunned executive, "Would you please help me get him back into his wheelchair? He's hurt and he's too heavy for me." Moved beyond words, the driver tried to swallow the rapidly swelling lump in his throat. He hurriedly lifted the disabled boy back into the wheelchair, then took out a linen handkerchief and dabbed at his fresh scrapes and cuts. A quick look told him everything was going to be okay. "Thank you," the grateful child told the stranger. Too shook up for words the man simply watched the boy push his wheelchair-bound brother down the path towards their home. It was a long, slow walk back to the Jaguar. The damage to the Jaguar was very noticeable, but the driver never bothered to repair the dented side door. He kept the dent there to remind him of this message: "Don't go through life so fast that someone has to throw a brick at you to get your attention!"

God often whispers in our ears and speaks to our hearts asking us to stop and be an Angel to those in need. Sometimes, when we don't have time to listen, when we're just too full of our own importance, He has no option but to throw a brick at us and shock us into stopping.

Reflection number 2

FLY LIKE AN EAGLE

One day, while he was out playing in the fields, a young boy made a strange find. He came upon an eagle's egg. For a joke, he decided to steal the eagle's egg and to place it into the hen's nest on the farm where he lived. In time, the eaglet hatched along with the hen's brood of chicks, and grew up alongside them.

All his life the eagle did what the farmyard chickens did, thinking that he himself was a chicken. Years passed and the eagle grew old. One day as he looked up, he saw a magnificent bird far above him in the clear blue sky. He watched it glide majestically above the powerful wind currents, with scarcely a beat of its strong golden wings. The old eagle looked in awe. "Who's that?" he asked one of the chickens who was standing there scratching the ground beside him. "That's the eagle, the king of the birds," said his neighbour. "He belongs to the sky. We're chickens—we belong to the earth." Eventually the old eagle died as he sat there clocking in the henhouse. He had been born alongside chickens, lived all his life with chickens and died in the company of chickens, for that's what he thought he was.

It's such a pity that so many of us are just like that poor old eagle in the story; we never quite reach our full potential. Every day in life we settle for so very little, and yet deep down we know that we're capable of so much more.

I remember as a wee fellow at school, we were told to reach for the moon, and at the very least you would land among the stars. All the boys in my class were putting up their hands and shouting out to the teacher that they wanted to be astronauts, film stars, prime ministers and presidents. I wonder where all those dreams went? What happened along the way?

It's never too late to follow your dream, no matter how old you think you are. We all need a dream, something to work towards, something to strive for, and something to hope for. It can be really hard at times, heading into the unknown, battling against all the odds, and facing all our fears and all our uncertainties, but hey, whoever said life was going to be a bowl of cherries?

Christopher Logue put it so beautifully when he wrote . . . "*Come to the edge. We might fall. Come to the edge. It's too high. Come to the edge. So they came, and we pushed, and they flew.*"

Reflection number 3

REVENGE! SWEET REVENGE!

A young Marine stationed in Afghanistan received a "Dear John" letter from his girlfriend back home. It read as follows:

'Dear Ricky, I can no longer continue our relationship. The distance between us is just too great. I must be honest and admit that I have also cheated on you twice since you've been gone, and that's not fair to either of us—I'm sorry. Please don't judge me, but understand that we are all human and all have very strong emotional needs. Kindly return the picture of me that I sent to you—love, Becky.'

With hurt feelings Ricky asked his fellow Marines for any snap shots they could spare of their girlfriends, sisters, ex-girlfriends, aunts and cousins etc. In addition to the photograph of Becky, Ricky included all the other pictures of the pretty gals that he had collected from his buddies. He posted home 57 photos in that envelope along with the following note:

'Dear Becky, I'm really sorry, but unfortunately I just can't seem to remember who you are. I have sincerely wracked my brain, but all sadly to no avail—Please take your picture from the pile, and kindly send the rest back to me—love, Ricky.'

Loving your neighbour, after they've hurt you, is very hard indeed. We live in an age where almost everyone wants to get "the last word", "the upper hand" and "their own back." A colossal amount of human energy is wasted every day on settling old scores and exacting vengeance—energy that surely could be put to so much better use.

Life is just not always going to be fair, and that's just the way life is—anyone who tells you any different is telling you lies. Thankfully the gospel recognises us as we are—sometimes petty, vengeful, unforgiving and on occasion even ruthless. Christ calls us to live another way, a better way, a healthier way, which involves letting go of past hurts and old wounds that steadily eat away at us like cancer if we choose to hold on to them.

Forgiveness is the preservative that keeps love from going bad—it also stops us all from becoming bitter, twisted, angry and contrary. Why not give it a go? If it's not your problem, then why hold on to it? An eye for an eye only leaves everyone blind, and who wants to spend their time growing old miserably, being avoided by people on the street because all we do is complain about how hard done by we are? Anyway, how can we possibly be happy, if we allow ourselves to be ruled by bitterness?

Enemies we will always have—the little ones prosecute us and the big ones persecute us. Letting go, and letting God take over the situation is a much better option—it's good for the mind, it's good for the body and it's good too for the soul. It's worth noting of course that it's also good for the world—makes it a much nicer and a much friendlier place for us all to live in! Worth trying?

Reflection number 4

IF YOU LOVE, TELL ME NOW!

The one thing in this world that touches all of us in one way or another is death! We feel many emotions as death leaves its mark with us. There is often sadness, loneliness, pain, emptiness, anger, shock and sometimes even regrets. Unfortunately there is no magic remedy or medication that will cure any of these feelings. They can never be got around; they can only be worked through.

I have always thought that wakes are fascinating places to visit. I find it amazing just to sit and look around me at all the different things that happen at a wake here in Ireland. The usual procedure for all those visiting a wake is to come into the room where the deceased is laid out. We shake one hand with the bereaved, and in the other hand we clasp a Mass card or a sympathy card. Very often this is our passport into the wake. Then we kneel down, say a prayer, put the sympathy card into the coffin, have a seat and generally make a comment like:—"Gosh he'll be sorely missed, yes he was one nice fella!" It's at times like this that I often think to myself that I would love to be lying there in the coffin just to hear what people would say about me, because really, it's one of the few times when we let our loved ones know how we truly feel about them.

It's a tremendous pity that in the course of each day we don't stop and take the time to tell people around us how special they are, and how much they mean to us. The cemeteries throughout Ireland are filled with beautiful headstones with beautiful tributes, all of which I have no doubt are true. But, why do we have to wait until people are dead, before we can pay these beautiful tributes to them?

A friend of mine gave me this wee reflection one day. It would be good if we could try and live it out.

If with pleasure you are viewing
Any work that I am doing
If you like me, or you love me, tell me now.
Don't withhold your approbation
Till the father makes oration
And I lie with snowy lilies o'er my brow.
For no matter how you shout it
I won't care much about it
I won't see how many teardrops you have shed.
If you think some praise is due me
Now is the time to slip it to me
For I cannot read my tombstone when I'm dead.
More than fame and more than money
Is the comment warm and sunny
Is the hearty approval of a friend.
For it gives to life a savour, and it makes me stronger, braver
And, it gives me spirit to the end.
If I earn your praise bestow it
If you like me let me know it
Let your words of encouragement be said.
Do not wait till life is over
And I'm underneath the clover
For I cannot read my tombstone when I'm dead.

Reflection number 5

ARE YOU JESUS?

One day a group of civil servants were making their way home after attending a computer conference. They were late, and they were all running across the platform of the train station, trying to make it on to the train that was just about to pull out of the station. In the mad rush, one of the men accidentally knocked into a table with apples on it. The apples went flying all over the place. All of the civil servants jumped on board the train, except for one girl who looked back. And when she looked back she saw a young boy sitting behind the table with apples scattered over the ground. He looked very sad.

The girl looked at the train moving off, but she still turned and walked over to the young boy to apologise. To her surprise, she saw that the boy was blind, and he told her that he was just sitting there waiting on his mother who had gone off to get them some sandwiches. The girl picked up the apples, stacked them up neatly, and put two that were damaged to one side. She then put her hand in her purse and gave the boy some money saying:—'Listen, I'm really sorry for what's happened. I certainly hope that we haven't ruined your day!' And as she turned to walk away, the young lad who was blind turned to her and said:—'Excuse me, are you Jesus?'

When we meet people in the course of our day, we never really know how they are feeling. So often people look as if everything's going just fine, and yet deep down they can be lonely, troubled, depressed, worried or even suicidal. There are so many people in our towns who walk about wearing masks. They have no one to talk to and there's no one to tell how they feel. That's why it's so important every day just to be nice, to be kind, to be friendly, to smile, to make the effort. It's an old saying that it's nice to be important, but it's more important to be nice! And if we do that, who knows—maybe some day we might even be mistaken for Jesus himself? It would certainly be the supreme compliment of all!

Reflection number 6

LIVING PENTECOST OUT EACH DAY

A Church in Scotland was looking for a new Minister. The Parish Selection Committee advertised the position in all the Church magazines. However, they were quite disappointed when only two Ministers applied for the job, and on top of this, the applicants were both female. The all-male committee invited the two female Ministers along to their Church and asked them to preach a selection of sermons. The committee listened, gave them marks out of ten, and after some lively discussion they selected a new Minister for their Parish Church. A very competent, well-educated, and very beautiful young woman was appointed. However, in truth all the men on the Parish Committee didn't really want a woman to be their Minister.

It had always been a tradition that the Chairman of the Parish Committee would go fishing along with the local Minister on Saturday morning. The same Chairman thought to himself that this woman wouldn't possibly be interested in fishing, but to his surprise whenever he broached the subject with her the new Minister said that she would be delighted to go. Early the next Saturday morning they both drove to the lake and once in the boat the Chairman rowed out across the water for about half a mile. Unfortunately the fishing that day was very bad. The lovely young Minister was very friendly and tried just about everything to get a conversation going. She started conversations around the subjects of fishing, families, holidays, work, weather, houses, cars, but no matter what she said, all she got was one-word answers. The temperature was dropping rapidly (and I'm not talking about the temperature in the water) and so the Minister announced that it was really time for her to go home, she had calls to make and people to visit and things to do. The Chairman of the committee responded by grunting, 'Fine. I'll row you back to shore.' However the Minister casually said, 'Not at all, there's no need for you to do that,' and she simply stepped out of the boat, walked across the lake, got into her car and drove back to the parish. The Chairman watched her walking on the water and muttered under his breath, 'some Minister that! Not only can she not fish, she can't swim either!'

The gifts of the Holy Spirit are love, joy, peace, patience, kindness, goodness, trustfulness, gentleness and self-control. Let's try and put them into practice as we begin each day, otherwise we simply can't call ourselves Christians!

Reflection number 7

I HAVEN'T GOT TIME

May I introduce you to the Tates?
First there is old man Dic-Tate, who wants to run everything, and his cousin Ro-Tate who wants to change everything around. Mrs. Agi-Tate stirs up trouble with her annoying husband Irri-Tate. When new ideas are suggested Mrs. Hesi-Tate and her husband Vege-Tate want to leave them to next year. Mrs. Imi-Tate wants everything to be like it was in her old parish and Mr. Devas-Tate is definitely a voice of doom, but I must say that Mr. Facili-Tate is most helpful. Mrs. Medi-Tate thinks all things over carefully, but poor Mrs. Ampu-Tate has cut herself off completely, and has no time for anyone!

The little phrase 'I haven't got time,' is one that we use most often ourselves and the one we hear most often from the people around us. It is the excuse we give for all of our failings and all of our shortcomings. We haven't time to call; we haven't time to write, and worse still, we haven't even time to answer letters that we have received from friends. It would seem that many of us have amputated ourselves from the people that we were once very close to, all because we have no time anymore. Not so long ago we used to describe the people that we didn't like by saying:—'I've no time for him, or I have no time for her.' It would appear nowadays, that we have no time even for those we love. Everyone now is in such a terrible rush.

What makes it all so remarkable is that we are living in an age when modern technology has furnished our lives and our homes with all sorts of time-saving gadgets. It is the age of instant coffee, the microwave dinners, and the mobile telephones (and for all of that some people still cannot get the time to ring home). If we just go back one generation to our parent's time and think about the days when modern timesaving implements were not available, our parents rarely if ever complained that they hadn't got time. On top of that they had much bigger families to attend to, and yet they always seemed to have plenty of time for everyone and everything. There is a lot of talk nowadays about the energy crisis, but I fear the real crisis facing us is not the shortage of oil, but the shortage of time.

I enclose an item that I cut out of a newspaper some years back. It's quite humorous but very challenging.

In a recent address to the House of Lords, the Archbishop of Canterbury used a small section from an essay written by a boy of eight. The essay contained the directness and the simplicity of a child and was entitled:—'What a granny is'.

A granny is a lady who has no children of her own, so she likes other peoples little girls and boys. A grandpa is a man granny. He goes for walks with boys and they talk about fishing and tractors.

Grannies don't have to do anything but be there. They are old so they shouldn't play hard or run. They never say 'hurry up'. Usually they are fat, but not too fat to tie children's shoes. They wear glasses and funny underwear and can take their teeth and gums off. They don't have to be smart, only answer questions like why dogs hate cats and why God isn't married. They don't talk baby talk like visitors. When they read to us they don't skip bits or mind if it is the same story over again. Everybody should have a granny, especially if you don't have television, because grannies are the only grown ups who have time!"

Interesting—Eh?

Reflection number 8

DEAR JOHN

If you go into a card shop nowadays you can buy a card for almost every occasion. There are get well cards, wishing you well cards, cards to say sorry and cards to tell someone you love them. I'm told that there is even a card available to send to your friend if he or she is going through a separation or a divorce. The words in all of these cards are certainly very beautiful, however, while a card telling you that someone loves you, or a card saying sorry is indeed very welcome, it's still a poor substitute for the real thing.

I remember a few years ago bumping into a friend of mine who was in the process of trying to break up with her boyfriend. No matter how hard she tried she just couldn't find the right words to explain how she was feeling, and here she was in a shop looking for a card that would do the job. 'It would be much easier' she explained to me, 'and much less painful for both of us'. I remember standing there in shock and saying, 'A card to end a relationship? Would you not be as well just to send him a tape of the song "Dear John"?'

From time to time we can all use the words on a card to get us out of an uncomfortable situation. We write our name and a message inside hoping that it will sort things out, because deep down we have neither the guts nor the words inside us to heal this awful situation that we have helped create. I've always thought that there is something very artificial about an apology that arrives in the post printed inside a card that was purchased from a shop.

Saint John in his Letter states, 'My children, our love is not to be just words or mere talk, but something real and active.' When it come to celebrating Fathers Day, let's try and do something more than just send a card that we have bought in a shop. Personally speaking, I would like to see the whole day being re-named 'Daddy's Day'—anyone can be a father, but it takes a very special kind of man to be a daddy! If you truly mean the words inside the card you hope to send, make sure that you tell them to your dad as well!

Reflection number 9

YOU ALWAYS CATCH MORE FLIES USING HONEY

One day, the sun and the wind were having a discussion. The question arose as to which of the two was the stronger. The wind maintained that he was more powerful and much more effective than the sun. The sun sat smiling and let the wind just blow away. The moon who happened to be listening in the background said it would be best to have a contest and that she would be only too happy to be the judge. Both parties agreed. They decided that a traveller upon the earth was to be the object of the experiment. Whoever could force the man to remove his coat would be judged the stronger of the two.

The wind made the first effort. As the traveller walked along feeling the steady pressure of the wind blowing upon him he wrapped his coat more securely around him and plodded on. The stronger the wind blew the tighter the traveller held on to his coat. Finally, it turned into a mighty gale but still the traveller clung to his coat, refusing to let go.

The moon called time and the sun took its turn. As it simply shone down upon the traveller, he immediately began to feel its effects. First he unbuttoned his coat but as the sun rose higher in the sky the heat was so beautiful that the traveller slipped off his coat and his jumper too. The sun was a clear winner.

The moral of the story is very simple. We can achieve just about anything in life if we use warmth, kindness and gentleness. If we want to be real Christians then we must remember that selfishness, roughness and aggressiveness should have no place in our lives. After all, they achieve nothing!

Reflection number 10

TO MY GROWN UP SON

The amazing thing about the summer holidays from school is that they seem to conjure up different emotions for all different ages. They are heaven for children, and at the other extreme, often hell for parents who by the time September arrives are almost ready to pull their hair out and commit infanticide. In the hot weather of July and August let's not forget the students, all those who are aspiring to reach distinction in their exams, and all the others who are perspiring heavily in the effort to avoid extinction!

My happiest memories of the summer holidays as a child was getting up early in the morning to watch Casey Jones on television as he went steaming and rolling along the railway tracks, always managing to save the world with the help of the Cannonball Express just before the final credits rolled. I suspect that children today would not be as easily taken in by Casey Jones or the adventures of Flash Gordon as I was. While the Multi-Coloured Swap Shop on Saturday morning has been replaced by much more hi-tech television such as Live and Kicking, and Noel Edmunds has been replaced with Ant and Dec, children are still the same today as ever before. They might wear clothes with designer labels, have their own mobile phone and surf the internet, but they still spell love with the same four letters—T.I.M.E.

One of my parishioners passed me this reflection going into Church one evening. Experience is always the best teacher of all. Perhaps through this mammy's experience we might learn to slow down a little bit more, and enjoy our children a whole lot more. It's quite simple really; all it involves is that magic word called 'time'.

My hands were busy through the day,
I didn't have much time to play
The little games you asked me to.
I didn't have much time for you.

I'd wash your clothes; I'd sew and cook,
But when you'd bring your picture book
And ask me, please to share your fun.
I'd say, 'A little later son.'

I'd tuck you in all safe at night,
And hear your prayers, turn out the light,
Then tiptoe softly to the door,
I wish now I'd stayed a minute more.

For life is short, and years rush past,
A little boy grows up so fast.
No longer is he at your side,
His precious secrets to confide.

The picture books are all put away.
There are no childrens games to play.
No goodnight kiss, no prayers to hear,
That all belongs to yesteryear.

My hands once busy, now lie still,
The days are long and hard to fill,
I wish I might go back and do,
All the little things you asked me to.

Reflection number II

A PRAYER FOR CHILDREN

As we read through the following prayer, let's try to relax and slow down, to enjoy the wonders of God's beautiful creation, and make sure that our children are always safe, secure, happy and loved!

> *I hope my children will look back on today*
> *And see a parent who had time to play*
> *There will be years ahead for cleaning and cooking*
> *Cause children grow tall when we're not looking*
> *So settle down cobwebs,*
> *Dust go to sleep,*
> *I'm cuddling my children*
> *Cos children don't keep!*

During holiday time the school gates around our country are all securely locked, and the playgrounds that were such kindred spirits to our children are sent to Coventry for two long months. However, when September eventually comes around, our children will have thought very seriously about Christ's commandment, 'love thy neighbour', and the bond of friendship with the poor old playground will once again be renewed. July and August are definitely enchanted. Children who have great difficulty getting up in the morning from January to June can now for some inexplicable reason rise at the crack of dawn. In twenty years time they will look back fondly on last summer and describe it as being filled with long, lazy, sultry days. Strange, isn't it, that you always think the summers of your childhood were endlessly warm and sunny?

It's important to ask God to watch over our children, not just in the holiday season but every day of their lives. Children should be happy, and if they're not there's something wrong. As we read through the following prayer let's remember children throughout the world, and let's always do our utmost to ensure that our own children always feel safe, happy and loved!

We pray for children
  Who sneak sweets before dinner,
  Who rub holes in their school books,
  Who can never find their socks.

And we pray for those
  Who stare at photographers from behind barbed wire,
  Who can't race down the street in a new pair of white runners,
  Who are born in places we wouldn't be caught dead in,
  Who never go to the circus,
  Who live in an 'X' rated world.

We pray for children
  Who bring us sticky kisses and fistfuls of dandelions,
  Who hug us in a hurry and forget their lunch money.

And we pray for those who never get dessert,
  Who have no safe blanket to drag behind them,
  Who watch their parents watch them die,
  Who can't find any bread to steal,
  Who don't have any rooms to clean up,
  Whose pictures aren't on anyone's dressing table,
  Whose monsters are real.

We pray for children
  Who spend all their pocket money before Tuesday,
  Who throw tantrums in the supermarket and pick at their food,
  Who like ghost stories,
  Who shove dirty clothes under the bed and never rinse out the sink,
  Who get visits from the tooth fairy,
  Who don't like to be kissed in front of the neighbours,
  Who squirm in church and scream on the phone,
  Whose tears we sometimes laugh at and whose smiles can make us cry.

And we pray for those
> *Whose nightmares come in the daytime,*
> *Who will eat anything,*
> *Who have never been seen by a dentist,*
> *Who aren't spoiled by anybody,*
> *Who go to bed hungry and cry themselves to sleep,*
> *Who live and move and have no being.*

We pray for children
> *Who want to be carried and those who must,*
> *For those we never give up on and those who don't get a second chance,*
> *For those whom we smother with love, and those who will grab the hand of anyone kind enough to offer it. Amen.*

Reflection number 12

COULD YOU JUST LISTEN?

A huge lorry with a heavy load got jammed under a bridge in the middle of a town. The traffic was backed up for miles in either direction. It was total chaos. An official from the company that owned the lorry finally arrived and made all kinds of attempts to help free it. School children gathered and sat on a wall nearby watching everything that was going on. A young lad shouted over to the official who looked so important as he stood there in his pinstriped suit, 'Hey Mister, do you want to know how to free the lorry?' 'No thank you' he replied, and muttered under his breath, 'All I need now is some young smart ass telling me how to do my job'. The young lad began to laugh and continued to sit on the wall with his many friends. Within a few hours the police and the fire brigade had all been called for, but with all their apparatus and collective expertise they were still unable to budge the lorry. The young lad made his way over to the company official again, and in front of all those standing there he asked, 'Do you think it might help if you let the air out of the tyres?'

The official began to shake his head. In his heart he knew that the air had been let out of his tyres, big time! The sad thing was that it could all have been avoided if he had only taken the time to listen to what someone else had to say.

It's worth noting that whenever God made man and woman he gave them two ears but only one mouth, and so by the law of averages we are expected to listen twice as much as we speak. It's hard to find good listeners today—everyone wants to be a Chief, no one wants to be an Indian. Let's try and put the following challenge into practice—but be warned, it's difficult to do!

When I ask you to listen to me and you start to give me advice,
You have not done what I asked.

When I ask you to listen to me
And you begin to tell me why I shouldn't feel that way,
You are trampling on my feelings.

When I ask you to listen to me
And you feel that you have to do something to solve my problem,
You have failed me, strange as that may seem.

Listen—
All I asked was that you listen,
Not talk or do—
Just hear me.

I can do for myself; I'm not helpless—
Maybe discouraged and faltering, but not helpless.

When you do something for me that I can and need to do for myself
You contribute to my fear and inadequacy.

Perhaps that's why prayer works,
Sometimes,
For some people—
Because God is mute,
And He doesn't give advice
He listens all the time and helps you work it all out for yourself.

So please listen and just hear me.

And if you want to talk, wait a minute for your turn—
And I'll listen to you.

Reflection number 13

BULLIES

Two battleships were out at sea in heavy weather on training manoeuvres. It was a dreadful evening and the visibility was very poor.

*The Captain stayed on the bridge keeping an eye on the activities going on around him. After dark the ship's lookout reported a light that was bearing on the starboard side. 'Is it steady or moving astern?' the Captain asked. 'Steady,' was the reply. The Captain called the signalman, 'Signal that ship. We are on a collision course. Advise **you** change course 20 degrees'. A signal came back 'Advise **you** change course 20 degrees.'*

*The Captain sent another signal, 'I'm a Captain. Change course 20 degrees.' A reply came back, 'I'm a seaman 2nd class. **You** had better change course 20 degrees.'*

The Captain was furious and spat out another message to be signalled, 'I'm a battleship! Change course 20 degrees!' A reply came back, 'I'm a lighthouse!' The Captain changed course 20 degrees.

Bullies are everywhere—they refuse to listen and they shout people down in order to get their own way. They walk over people at work, at home, at school and in the community. They are vexation to the spirit, and they constantly deride and humiliate—we've all met them at some stage in life. But, just like the Captain on the battleship, they are cowards when they eventually meet someone who stands up to them and faces them head on.

Christ was never afraid to stand up for what was right in the face of all types of adversity. He openly criticised and challenged those who made life difficult for others, and he preached a beautiful message of equality and compassion. He suggested that rather than power and authority giving us freedom, it is always the truth that sets us free.

Nelson Mandela used the following reflection in his inaugural speech in 1994. Mandela was a self-educated prisoner of conscience who was to become South Africa's port in the storm. He was the man who faced all the bullies and won. If we take anything from Mandela or this reflection he chose when he became South Africa's first black president, let it be that we will never ever let anyone bully us, or walk over us in life!

Our deepest fear
Is not that we are inadequate.
Our deepest fear
Is that we are powerful beyond measure.
It is our light, not our darkness that most frightens us.
We ask ourselves, Who am I to be brilliant,
Gorgeous, talented and fabulous?
Actually, who are you not to be?
You are a child of God
Your playing small doesn't serve the world.
There is nothing enlightened about shrinking
So that other people won't feel insecure around you.
We were born to manifest
The glory of God within us.
It is not just in some of us, it's in everyone.
And, as we let our own light shine,
We unconsciously give other people
Permission to do the same.

As we are liberated from our own fear,
Our presence automatically liberates others.

Reflection number 14

THE NURSERY SCHOOL

When my nephew Ronan was leaving Nursery School his teacher gave him this reflection to pin up in his bedroom. I don't think it stayed up on the wall too long. As the years went by posters of W.W.F. wrestlers replaced it, and just last week I heard my sister Kathleen mention that Rachael, Monica and Phoebe from 'Friends' immediately smile at him every time he opens the door into his room.

As he grows up I hope that he will manage to get his hands on this reflection again. It's written for children all right, but it's a great guide for both children and adults to live their lives by.

Most of what I really need to know about how to live, and what to do, and how to be, I learned at the nursery school. Wisdom was not at the top of the university mountain, but there in the sand pit.

These are the things I learned.

Share everything. Play fair. Don't hit people. Put things back where you found them. Clean up your own mess. Don't take things that aren't yours. Say sorry when you've hurt someone. Wash your hands before you eat. Live a balanced life. Learn a bit and think a bit, and draw and sing and play and work every day.

Take a nap in the afternoon, when you go out into the world, watch for traffic, hold hands and stick together. Be aware of wonder. Remember the little seed in the plastic cup. The roots go down and the plant goes up, and nobody really knows why, but we are all like that.

Goldfish and hamsters and white mice and even the little seed in the plastic cup—they all die. So do we!

And then remember one of the first words you learned to read, the biggest word of all: **look**.

Think what a better world it would be if we all had biscuits and milk about three o'clock every afternoon and then lay down with our blankets for a nap. Or if we had a basic policy to always put things back where we found them and cleaned up our own messes. And it is still true, no matter how old you are, when you go out into the world, it is best to hold hands and stick together.

Reflection number 15

GO PICK SOME DAISIES

It's so important to constantly remind ourselves that we only get one go at life. When Jesus said, 'I have come that they may have life and life to the full' (*John 10:10*)—he definitely meant it! Sadly there are some people who are under the illusion that they are living life to the full, not realising that in actual fact they are destroying their very lives every day by the way they live.

I remember calling into a Church in Dublin one day to say a few prayers, and while on my knees I noticed a colourful poster inviting parishioners of all ages to come along to a bible study group. The group wasn't made up of scripture scholars or theologians, but simple honest to God people who read their bible every day, who tried their best to interpret it, and then put it into practice. The poster began, 'Does the following sum up your life? Youth—a disaster? Middle Age—A Big Effort? Old Age—Regrets?'

If we fit into one of those categories, I think it's safe to say that we are definitely doing something wrong, because when God made us, he made us to be happy. In the age of high blood pressure, coronary disease, early retirements through ill health and a plethora of other sad and stressful situations we might like to take advice from a woman of eighty who wrote the following reflection as she looked back on her life with some regret. Remember, we only get one go at life—so be sure to make the most of it!

If I had my life to live all over again, I'd begin by trying to make more mistakes next time around. I would relax. I would lighten up. I would be sillier than I had been on this trip. I know of very few things that I would take seriously. I would be crazier. I would take more chances. I would take more holidays. I would sing and dance and praise God much more.

I would climb more mountains, swim more rivers and watch more sunsets. I would eat more ice cream and less carrots. I would have more actual troubles and fewer imaginary ones.

You see, I am one of those people who lives life slowly and sensibly and sanely, hour after hour, day after day. Oh, I have my moments and, if I had to do it all over again, I'd make sure that I'd have many more of them. In fact I'd try and have nothing else, just moments, one after another, instead of living so many years ahead each day.

I am one of those people who never goes out anywhere without a thermometer, a hot water bottle, an umbrella, a raincoat, a parachute and a map giving directions to the nearest hospital.

If I had my life to live over, I would start barefooted earlier in the spring and stay that way later in the fall. I would play hooky from school and work more often. I wouldn't make such good grades, except by accident. I would swing on more swings and ride on more merry go-rounds, and most important of all, **I'd pick more daisies***!*

Reflection number 16

SMILE—JESUS LOVES YOU (AND SO DO I)

I came across this thought-provoking reflection a while back. It has a simple but very effective message and is called 'The Meaning of a Smile'. It goes like this . . .

It costs nothing, but it creates much.
It enriches those who receive
Without impoverishing those who give.
It happens in a flash, but the memory of it lasts forever.
None are so rich that they can get along without it
And none are so poor but are richer for its benefit.
It creates happiness in the home, fosters good will in a business
And is the countersign of friends.
It is rest to the weary, daylight to the discouraged,
Sunshine to the sad and nature's best antidote for trouble;
Yet it cannot be begged, bought, borrowed or stolen,
For it is something that is of no earthly use to anyone, until it is given away.
So, in the course of the day
If some of your friends are too tired to give you a smile,
Why don't you give them one of yours?
For nobody needs a smile so much
As those who have none left to give.

Today there is much said and written about suicide. As priests we get the opportunity so often to meet with, and listen to people who have attempted suicide, and also to work with families who have lost a loved one because of suicide. I always thought that it's so important for us to smile, and smile often in the course of the day; because whenever we meet people we never really know what personal pain they may be going through. A simple smile, a few words of encouragement can make such a difference in a person's life!

I remember visiting a friend of mine in hospital a few years back, just after he had attempted suicide. He explained that he just couldn't take anymore of this life. For him there was no light. All he could see was darkness and all he could feel was pain, pain and more pain. It's so important in life no matter where we are, to listen, to care and to be nice to those around us—God only knows what they might be going through. I don't think any of us could ever understand the mind of someone who feels suicidal unless we ourselves have been in that position. However, even if we don't know what it feels like, there are many ways in which we can help. We could join the Samaritans or another 'help' organisation. We could be good listeners—the world needs good listeners. We could be nice to the people we meet every day, and at all times we can try our best not to judge.

The one thing to remember at all times is that help is available for everything and for everyone. There are organisations to help you if you are having problems with exams, with loneliness, with bereavement, with worry or anxiety. There are wonderful groups to help victims of abuse, children who are being bullied, people who are homeless, anyone who is poor, families who are in crisis, those who suffer from addictions to alcohol, gambling, and narcotics, for those who have an unplanned pregnancy and those who need post-abortion counselling.

There is help for everything; however, in order to get help, you have to take the first step and reach out for it. Lift the telephone, call the Samaritans, call a member of your family, call a friend, call your priest, call your minister, just call someone! There is no problem that cannot be worked out.

A mother from a former parish of mine wrote this letter not long after she lost her son, and she asked me to read it out in Church wherever I would go. Please God it may be of some help to someone!

To anyone who has ever contemplated taking their own life, this is a heartfelt message from the parents of a child who did.

Please do not feel that you are alone with your worries. We beg you to seek help from someone who loves you, your father or mother, your sister or brother, your husband or wife, your priest, your minister, your teacher, or a good friend you can confide in. Someone will always be willing to help you and give you the consolation and support that you need.

Our child is gone, and we know that he didn't mean to hurt us. We love him just the same. He was not to know the grief that we would suffer at his loss. Words cannot begin to describe our grief and that of our family. Trust in God is our only consolation.

Please, we beg you, do not cause your loved ones to suffer in this way. Give them the chance to help you. Do not be afraid. There is someone who will ease your burden and console you. You are not alone. Do not lose hope.

Reflection number 17

SO JUST HOW LUCKY ARE YOU?

If Earth's population were shrunk into a village of just 100 people, with all the human ratios of the world still remaining, what would this tiny, diverse village look like?

That's exactly what Phillip M. Harter, a medical doctor at the Stanford University School of Medicine, attempted to figure out. This is what he found:

57 would be Asian
21 would be European
14 would be from the Western Hemisphere
8 would be African
52 would be female
48 would be male
70 would be non white
30 would be white
70 would be non-Christian
30 would be Christian
89 would be heterosexual
11 would be homosexual
6 people would possess 59 percent of the entire world's wealth, and all 6 would be from the United States.
80 people would live in substandard housing and
70 would be unable to read
50 people would suffer from malnutrition
1 would be near death
1 would be pregnant
1 would have a college education.

The following is an anonymous interpretation: *If you live in a good home, have plenty to eat and can read, you are a member of a very select group. And if you have a good house, food, can read and have a computer, you are among the very elite. If you woke up this morning with more health than illness . . . you are more fortunate than the million people who will not survive this week. If you have never experienced the danger of battle, the loneliness of imprisonment, the agony of torture or the pangs of starvation . . . you are ahead of 500 million people in the world. If you can attend a church meeting without fear of harassment, arrest, torture, or death . . . you are fortunate, more than three billion people in the world can't.*

If you have food in the refrigerator, clothes on your back, a roof overhead and a place to sleep . . . you are richer than 75% of this world. If you have money in the bank, in your wallet, and spare change in a dish someplace . . . you are among the top 8% of the worlds wealthy.

If your parents are still alive and still married . . . you are very rare indeed. If you hold up your head with a smile on your face and are truly thankful . . . you are blessed, because although the majority can, most do not.

If you can hold someone's hand, hug them or even touch them on the shoulder . . . you are blessed, because you can offer a healing touch.

If you can read this message, you have just received a double blessing in that someone was thinking of you, and furthermore, you are more blessed than over two billion people in the world that cannot read at all.

Still feel like moaning?

Reflection number 18

EXPLAIN TO ME HOW YOU SHOWED LOVE?

On a cold miserable winter's day an old man came upon a small boy sitting alone on the ground on a wind-swept city bridge. The boy was shivering, and was obviously in need of a good hot meal. On seeing the young boy the man got very angry and shouted at God:

'Lord, why don't you do something about this boy?'
God replied, 'I have done something about him.'
This surprised the man greatly, and in his anger he said to God, 'I hope you don't mind me saying this, but whatever you did, it's clearly not working. There are so many people in this world either starving or suffering.'
'I agree with you there,' God replied, 'my whole plan just seems to be failing.'
'Really?' the man roared, 'what exactly did you do?'
'I made you!' came the reply.

It's okay to ask God to put right all the wrongs in the world, and to comfort all those who are suffering, but what we must remember is that God can only do all those things if we help him out. We might think:—what difference can I make? Well, quite a lot if we're really prepared to make the effort!

There's a true story told about an unemployed couple who lived in Dallas, Texas. They were very poor, and in order to get some money to live on, they went around the city early each morning collecting aluminium beer tins which they sold for recycling. As part of their daily work they had to search through many bins and filthy alleyways. One morning they made a very sad discovery when they found the body of a newborn baby lying inside an old dustbin. The couple immediately reported it to the police, however the police were unable to trace the parents of the child, and with no parents, there was no one to bury the baby. The same couple wanted so much to give the baby a decent funeral, but they knew this would cost money, and they had very little. So, the woman pawned her engagement ring along with her wedding ring to help pay for the funeral expenses.

Thanks to their efforts the baby went to its final resting-place in a little white coffin with fresh white flowers. At the funeral, the tears shed by the couple were as pure as those shed by Jesus at the grave of his friend Lazarus.

If we want to be a source of light to those around us, the first thing we'll need is a warm heart followed by a willingness to let it warm others who suffer from the cold. In a world where so much value is placed on jobs, houses and possessions, Jesus invites all of us to be apostles, and we can do this by simply caring for people in need. Whenever we meet God on the last day, and we're all going to meet God on the last day, I imagine that his first question might be: 'Now, explain me how you showed love to all the people around you?'

What do you think you'll say in reply?

Reflection number 19

GET YOUR OWN HOUSE IN ORDER FIRST

One day an old monk and a young novice were out walking around the grounds of the monastery. As they walked along the old monk instructed the young novice about commitment to God and to monastic life. The young novice asked many questions. In the distance both of them could see a river, and a beautiful young woman standing there at the edge of the water. As they approached the young woman asked the monks if they could help, as she needed to get across the water to the bank on the other side. There was no bridge anywhere around and she was afraid of being swept away in the strong current. The older monk smiled, picked the young woman up in his arms, waded through the water with her, and sat her down on the other side. The woman was ever so grateful and she thanked the monk profusely. The monk crossed back over to the other side and headed towards the monastery with the young novice. The novice was very quiet. As they reached the monastery the novice asked the old monk if he was going to tell the Abbot about the fact that he had picked up a beautiful young woman in his arms and carried her across the river? The old monk smiled and asked why would he need to do that? 'Well,' said the novice, 'Do you think it's right and proper for a monk who has taken a vow of chastity to lift a beautiful girl and carry her in his arms in the way that you did?' The old monk laughed and said, 'the big difference between you and me is, I only picked the girl up and then I sat her down at the other side of the river. One hour later you are still carrying her in your mind!'

How often do we go out of our way to be petty about those around us? Christianity has always suffered from an abundance of holy people and a shortage of whole people. It's so easy to criticise others and become scathing in our remarks, without seeing the 'bigger picture'.

Isn't it just great whenever we try to find faults in others? It's great because it stops us having any time to look at ourselves.

A young businessman began to date a charming young actress. The relationship progressed and developed until it reached the point where the businessman was considering the possibility of marrying her. Being a very cautious businessman, he hired a private detective to check out the young actress, to ensure that there were no skeletons in her cupboard.

The detective knew nothing of the relationship; in fact, all he had been given was the young woman's name, which was passed to him by a friend of a friend. His investigation was very thorough indeed, and he submitted his findings in writing. They read: 'This is a very charming, honest and upright young lady. There seems to be but one blemish on her character. It appears that, of late, she has been keeping company with a young businessman of very doubtful character, and of questionable reputation.'

—*Hypocrite! First rid the beam out of your own eye, and then you can see the speck in your brother's eye.' (Matthew. 7:5)*

Reflection number 20

THE PARABLE OF THE PRESENT

A wealthy man and his son loved to collect rare works of art. They had everything in their collection, from Picasso to Raphael, Constable and da Vinci.

When war broke out the son felt that it was his duty to go and fight. He was very courageous in battle, but was killed rescuing another soldier. When the father was notified about his son's death he was inconsolable.

Some months later, a knock came to the father's door. A young man stood there with a large package in his hands. He said, 'you don't know me, sir, but I am the soldier for whom your son gave his life. He saved many lives that day, and he was carrying me to safety when a bullet struck him in the heart. He died instantly. He often talked about you and your great love of art. We were great friends!'

The young man held out a package; 'I know this isn't much,' he said, 'I'm not what you would call a great artist, but I think your son would have liked this and would have wanted you to have it'.

The father opened the package. It was a portrait of his son painted by the young man. He stared in awe at the way the soldier had captured the complete personality of his son in his painting. The father was so drawn to the eyes that his own soon welled up with huge tears. He thanked the young man and offered to pay him for the painting.

'Oh no sir, I could never repay what your son did for me. It's a gift.'

The father hung the portrait over the mantle. Every time visitors came to the home, he took them to see the portrait before he would show them any of the great works of art by the old masters.

In time, the father himself died. Without any family or heirs, there was to be an auction of the paintings. Many influential people gathered, excited to see the great paintings, and to have an opportunity to buy one for their own collections.

Behind the auctioneers platform hung the painting of the man's son. The auctioneer pounded the gavel. 'We shall commence the sale with bids on this portrait of the son. Who will bid for the picture?'

There was silence.

Then a voice from the gathered audience shouted out, 'We want to see the famous paintings. Skip this one'.

The auctioneer persisted. 'Will someone bid for this painting? Who will start the bidding at £200.00 . . . or £100.00 then?'

Another voice shouted, 'We didn't come to buy this painting . . . We came for the Van Goughs, the Rembrandts. Get on with the real sale!'

But the auctioneer persisted, 'The son! The son! Who will take the son?' . . . He paused, 'Who will start the bidding at all?'

Finally, a quiet voice came from the very back of the auction room. It was the long time gardener of the man and his son. 'I'll give you £10.00 for the painting'. Being a poor man it was all he could afford.

'We have a £10.00 bid, who will bid £20.00?' said the auctioneer.

'Give it to him for the £10.00.' 'Lets see the masters' came another shout from the crowded hall.

£10.00 is the bid, will someone bid £15.00?'

The crowd became very irritated; they didn't want the picture of the son. The wanted the more wealthy investments for their collections.

The auctioneer pounded the gavel . . . 'Going once, twice . . . and SOLD for £10.00'.

A man sitting in the second row shouted, 'Now let's get on with the collection!'

The auctioneer laid down his gavel. 'I'm sorry' he said, 'the auction is over'.

'But what about the other paintings, the old masters?'

'I'm sorry. When I was called upon to conduct this auction, I was given a secret and strict instruction stipulated in the will. I was not allowed to reveal that stipulation until this time. Only the painting of the son would be auctioned. Whoever bought the painting of the son would inherit the entire estate, including all the other paintings. The person who gets the son gets everything!'

God gave his son 2000 years ago to die on a cruel cross. Much like the auctioneer, God's message today is, 'The son! The son! Who will take the son?' Because, you see, whoever takes the son, gets everything!

Reflection number 21

YOU'RE RICH AND YOU DON'T KNOW IT

Just imagine that there is a bank situated beside your home, and every morning it credits your personal account with £86,400.00. Unfortunately it carries no balance over from one day to the next, as each night it deletes whatever amount of money you failed to spend. How would you live out your day with such a magnanimous gift?

Each one of us has our own personal bank. It's called 'The Time Bank', and each morning it credits our lives with 86,400 seconds. Each night it writes off as lost whatever time we fail to invest in a good purpose. It carries over no balance and allows no over-draught. If we fail to use the day's deposit, the loss is ours; there is no going back. But each morning it opens up a brand new account for us, no matter how good or bad we may have lived the day before. We get so many chances.

However, it's important for us never to waste the precious gift of time that God gives to us each day. We must all realise that there will surely come a day when our lives will not be credited with any more time.

Time is priceless! If you want to realise the value of one year, ask a student who has just failed an exam? To realise the value of one month, ask a mother who gave birth to a premature baby? To realise the value of one day, ask a daily wage labourer with kids to feed? To realise the value of one minute, ask a person who has just missed the train? To realise the value of one second, ask a person who has just avoided an accident? And to realise the value of one milli-second, ask the person who won the silver medal in the Olympics?

Let's spend our time wisely, because no doubt we'll all have to account for it on the final day!

Reflection number 22

LOOKING INTO THE MIRROR

There's a story told about an old farmer and his wife who had been married for a very long time. Sadly they had no family, and throughout the course of their day they barely spoke to one another except to grunt or to pass a comment that was usually cutting or negative. One morning the farmer was going to town to buy some cattle when he happened to meet a pedlar. The pedlar was selling just about everything, and he tried to talk the farmer into buying a mirror. The farmer had never seen a mirror before and whenever the pedlar showed him what he looked like in the mirror he was astounded. He couldn't believe how old and tired and dirty looking he was, and so he decided there and then that he would do something to improve his appearance. After buying the mirror he took it home and hid it in the attic.

Every afternoon the farmer would climb into the attic and looked at himself in his mirror, and as the time went past he made sure that his hair was washed and cut regularly and that he combed it several times throughout every day. He began to shave first thing every morning and take greater care of his skin and his teeth. After a while the farmer liked what he saw in the mirror.

However, while all this was going on his wife was beginning to get very suspicious, and one day when he was milking the cows she climbed into the attic and found his mirror. Unfortunately she had never seen a mirror before either, and whenever she looked at it she immediately thought it was a photograph of his fancy woman. 'Well' she said, 'Such a sour old blade I've never seen the like of before, and to think that he's coming up here to look at her face every day!'

The farmer's wife set off to tell the local priest her sad story. However, whenever she arrived at the parochial house she discovered that the priest had gone out on a sick call. The farmer's wife left the mirror with the priest's housekeeper and said that she would return to talk to the priest later. Whenever the priest returned home his housekeeper informed him that the local farmer's wife had called and that she had left a message for him on the hall table. The priest also had never seen a mirror before and whenever he looked at it he thought he was seeing a photograph of the neighbouring priest. 'My goodness', he said to himself, 'Such a wizened up old face. Surely the bishop should have retired that old man years ago.'

The story goes on and on, but the message behind it is very simple, sometimes when we all look closely at ourselves we don't like what we see—and in this case I'm not talking about something that the Oil of Olay can cure. There are many people in our parishes all around who have low self-esteem; who are not good at accepting compliments and who feel that they have nothing to give. In some cases this can be due to the way that they have been brought up as children, or perhaps it's because they have listened for years to family members or work colleagues continually putting them down.

This self-esteem creed was written for young people. However, it doesn't matter what age we are, if we could try and put it into practice in our own lives every day it would do wonders for our self-confidence.

'God made me—I was no accident.
I was in God's plan and he doesn't make junk, ever.
I was born to be a successful human being,
I am someone special, unique, definitely one of a kind. And I love me.
That is essential so that I might love you too.
I have talents, potentials, yes, there is greatness in me,
And, if I harness that specialness,
then I will write my name with my deeds . . . .
I was born in God's image and likeness.
And I will strive to do God's will.'

Reflection number 23

DRINK, GIRLS . . . .

In the city of Dub, there's a popular pub
All soft coloured lighting within.
And you'll find there a dame who is known by the name
Of 'Miss doesn't know where to begin.'

She's completely teetotal, and she's willing to quote all
Her reasons for total abstaining;
But she'll join you for one lest the feelings of some
Should be hurt by her rudely refraining.

She would like a small whiskey, only whiskey's so risky,
And the same can be said for a gin;
Rum and cocktails are out, and she doesn't like stout,
So she doesn't know where to begin.

At last she begins with the smallest of gins,
Then the small ones get bigger and bigger,
But she doesn't mind that, for they talk through their hat
When they say that gin ruins your figure.

She begins to feel strange, so she says that she'll change,
And her next is a whiskey and soda;
When the next round has come, she changes to rum.
For one whiskey was always her quota.

By now she looks weary, eyes a little bit bleary,
And she thinks that the whole world adores her.
She makes no demands on a man when he stands,
She'll drink any darn thing that he pours her.

'Time gentlemen, please,' finds her weak at the knees,
And she needs something strong to support her,
So she has just one more, and she heads for the door,
Fully armed with her bottle of porter.

Then two gallant men drag her home once again,
And present her to Momma and Pop!
And by general acclaim, they are changing her name;
To 'Miss doesn't know where she should stop!'

I've always thought that if anyone has money to invest and they're looking for quick return; invest it immediately in an Off License or a Public House. Public Houses never ever seem to be empty, and around towns and cities there's no end to the amount of people on their way home with their blue plastic bags.

A friend of mine who teaches in a post-primary school told me that some years back a few teachers brought a group of around thirty young people to France for a week. While it was a holiday it was also a chance for the young people to become accustomed to the French language and culture. Whenever they arrived they were brought to the hostel where they were to stay. In the kitchen area of the hostel there was a very large refrigerator that was filled with a selection of wines and orange juices. The director of the hostel had filled the fridge as a gesture of hospitality. Before the end of that first night the fridge was completely empty!

It might be good to ask ourselves why do we drink so much? And secondly, why do we have to drink so quickly? Some people say that alcohol is a curse. Alcohol is not a curse—the abuse of alcohol is a curse. Total abstinence was never intended except for the heroic few. The rest of us are simply called to moderation. To quote an old moralist—'moderation is not only a virtue, it enhances the quality of our lives!'

Reflection number 24

A LIVING HEAVEN OR A LIVING HELL?

Story number one—*Late one night a village blacksmith had a vision. An angel appeared to him and said, 'The Lord has sent me to take you home.' 'Well, I certainly thank God for thinking of me,' said the blacksmith, 'but as you know, the people from the village will need their ploughs repaired and their horses shod. I don't want to seem ungrateful, but do you think I might put off taking up my home in God's kingdom until I've finished?' The angel simply smiled and said, 'I'll see what can be done.' The blacksmith continued with his work and was almost finished when he heard of a neighbour who fell ill. The next time he saw the angel, the blacksmith pointed towards the barren fields and pleaded with the angel, 'Do you think eternity can hold off for just a little longer? If I don't finish this job, my friend's family will suffer.' Again the angel smiled and left. The blacksmith's friend recovered, but then another neighbour's barn burnt down. Whenever the angel reappeared, the blacksmith just spread his hands in a gesture of compassion and drew the angel's eyes to where the suffering was.*

One evening the blacksmith began to feel very old and tired, and in his prayers he said, 'Lord, if you would like to send your angel again, I think I would like to see him now.' He had no sooner spoken than the angel stood before him. 'If you still want to take me,' said the blacksmith; 'I am ready now to take up my place in the kingdom of God.' The angel looked at the blacksmith in surprise and smiled saying, 'And where do you think you have been all these years?'

Story number two—*A foolish man died and was brought to a most luxurious palace. Whenever he felt hungry a personal servant appeared before him with most exotic foods. Whenever he was thirsty the servant appeared again with many delightful cocktails for him to sample, and* whenever he was tired a deluxe four-poster bed appeared out of nowhere. This procedure of receiving opulent gifts went on for a very long time until the man eventually stopped his servant and asked, 'Does this procedure of just constantly taking go on for all eternity?' 'Oh yes, it certainly does,' he replied. The man put his head in his hands and sighed, 'Oh Lord, I can't take this any longer, I think I'd be better off in hell!' The servant began to laugh mockingly at him. He then folded his arms and asked, 'Just where exactly do you think you are?'

What kingdom are you living in?

Reflection number 25

A ROOM WITH THE VIEW

Two men who were both seriously ill lay in the same small hospital room. The room had only one window. The first man who was called John, could move slightly, and once a day he was allowed to sit up in his bed which was placed right next to the window. On these occasions John would look out at the world and smile—he was such a lovely old gentleman. The man in the bed opposite was called Peter, and he had to spend all his time lying on the flat of his back—he complained constantly about everything and everyone.

Every afternoon as John sat up he would pass the time describing to his roommate what he could see outside. The window apparently overlooked a park where there was a lake. There were ducks and swans in the lake, and children came to throw them bread and to sail model boats. Young lovers walked hand in hand beneath the trees, and there were flowers, stretches of grass, games of football, and at the back, behind the ring of trees there was a fine view of the city skyline.

John patiently described all of this to Peter to help lift his spirits. He told him how a child nearly fell into the lake, how lovely the girls were, and he depicted all kinds of adventuresome things to pass the time away. Peter could almost feel he was there in the park. Then one afternoon a dark thought hit him. Why should the man next to the window have all the pleasure of seeing what was going on? Why shouldn't he get the chance? It wasn't fair. He tried to stifle such thoughts, but each day, like Saul's jealousy of David, they became stronger and soured his soul. Something had to change.

One night as he lay with his thoughts, staring at the ceiling, John suddenly woke up. He coughed and choked and tried to reach for the button that would bring the nurse running. Peter watched all of this from his bed and managed to push the emergency button just slightly out of his reach.

In the morning, the nurse found John dead and quietly took his body away. As soon as it seemed decent, Peter asked if he could be switched to the bed close to the window. The nurses moved him, tucked him in, and made him comfortable.

The minute they left, Peter propped himself up on one elbow and looked out of the window. It faced a blank wall!

Jealousy and envy are foul things, and only serve to lead us down a pathway of self-destruction!

Reflection number 26

HALLOWEEN

An eighty-five year old widow went on a blind date with a ninety year old man. When she returned to her daughter's house later that night, she seemed upset. 'What happened mother?' the daughter asked. 'Well, I had to slap his face three times during our date' the mother said. 'You mean he tried to get fresh with you?' the daughter cried. 'No,' she answered, 'I thought he was dead!'

Although it's not Halloween until tomorrow, the bangers and the firecrackers have been going off for weeks now. At one stage recently I thought I was living in the middle of a war zone. We blame young people so often for noise and destruction, but do the shop owners who sell these horrible bangers not realise that in our town live old people, sick people, children and babies? There are people in hospital and in the hospice, people receiving chemotherapy and radium treatment, people suffering from depression, people who are pregnant and people who are in mourning and who live all alone. Not all the senior citizens in our parish can go out on dates like the lady in the story above. The majority of them are housebound, and the very least that they and everyone else around our parish want is simple peace and quiet!

If you're a young person, please think twice before you buy these bangers. If you're a parent—check what your children are up to. And if you're a shopkeeper perhaps you might ask yourself is there a better way of making a few pounds than this?

I found this wee prayer pinned up on the notice board of a local hospital. It's called 'Beatitudes for the Elderly.' Let's think long and hard about our senior citizens this Halloween and let's give them the respect, peace and quietness they so rightly deserve.

Blessed are you who understand that my feet falter and my hand is unsteady.

Blessed are you who understand that my ears are dull and so I don't always catch what you say.

Blessed are you who understand that my eyes are dim and my thoughts confused.

Blessed are you who understand the meaning of a friendly smile and the joy of a little chat.

Blessed are you who understand how precious certain memories are to me.

Blessed are you who never say you have told me that twice today.

Blessed are you who understand my loneliness and come to keep me company.

Blessed are you who are good to me and make happy those few days remaining in my journey towards eternity!

Reflection number 27

FAIR IS FAIR

Story number one—*Christian Herter was running for re-election as governor of the State of Massachusetts. One evening during his campaign he arrived late at a barbecue. The whole morning and afternoon had been hectic with shaking hands, begging for votes and making political promises. Unfortunately Mr Herter hadn't had a chance to eat that day, and by now he was totally famished. As he moved along the serving line he held out his plate and received one piece of chicken. The governor looked down at his plate and said to the serving lady, 'Pardon me, but would you mind if I have another piece of chicken? I'm very hungry.' The woman replied, 'I'm sorry sir, we have only so much food to go around, and I'm only supposed to give one piece of chicken to each person.' Herter repeated, 'But I'm starving, and I haven't had a chance to eat all day with the campaign being so busy.' Again the woman said, 'I'm sorry sir. Only one piece of chicken per customer.'*

Now Herter was normally a modest man, but decided that this was definitely the time to use the weight of his office. 'Madam,' he said, 'Do you know who I am? I am the governor of the state of Massachusetts.' The woman looked blandly into his face, and as she held her serving tongs in her hand she said, 'And do you know who I am? I'm the lady in charge of the chicken! Now move along mister!'

While it must be very nice to be important, I suspect that it's more important to be nice. The thing to remember about equality is that it's supposed to apply to absolutely everyone!

Story number two—*In a certain town a local bank tried to help married students with their financial problems. As it was a university town, they hired as many male students wives as they possibly could.*

However, a problem arose for the bank officials when some of the students' wives became pregnant, and they stayed on the job longer than the bank officials would have preferred. Eventually the bank adopted a ridiculous rule that required pregnant women periodically to stand against a certain wall, and when the time came that any part of their anatomy touched the opposite wall, they would have to leave their jobs.

One of the women was so incensed at this indignity that she went to the national Labour Relations Board and claimed unfair discriminatory tactics. The Board agreed with her and ruled that this same test would have to be applied equally to all employees.

As a result the bank lost two students wives and three male vice-presidents.

Reflection number 28

LIFE'S LITTLE LESSONS

If we haven't learned some of these lessons already, let's try and make a start . . . .

I've learned that the best classroom in the world is just sitting at the feet of an elderly person.

I've learned that when you're in love with someone it shows, and when you're not in love it also shows.

I've learned that just one person saying to me, 'You've made my day', makes my day.

I've learned that having a child fall asleep in your arms is one of the most peaceful feelings in the world.

I've learned that being kind is more important than being right.

I've learned that I can always pray for someone when I don't have the strength to help them in some other way.

I've learned that no matter how serious life requires you to be, everyone needs a friend to have a laugh with.

I've learned that sometimes all a person needs is a hand to hold and a heart to understand.

I've learned that life is like a roll of toilet paper. The closer it gets to the end the faster it goes.

I've learned that we should be glad God doesn't give us everything we ask for.

I've learned that money doesn't buy class.

I've learned that small daily happenings make life spectacular.

I've learned that underneath a person's hard shell is someone who wants to be appreciated and loved.

I've learned that the Lord didn't do it all in one day. What makes me think I can?

I've learned that to ignore the facts does not change the facts.

I've learned that when you plan to get even with someone, you are only letting that person continue to hurt you.

I've learned that love, not time heals all wounds.

I've learned that no one is perfect until you fall in love with them.

I've learned that life is tough, but I'm tougher.

I've learned that when you harbour bitterness, happiness will dock elsewhere.

I've learned that I should keep my words both soft and tender, because tomorrow I may have to eat them.

I've learned that a smile is a very inexpensive way to improve your looks.

I've learned that I can't choose how I feel, but I can choose what I do about it.

I've learned that everyone wants to live on the top of the mountain, but all the happiness and growth occurs when you're actually climbing the mountain.

I've learned that it is best to give advice in only two circumstances; when it is requested and when it is a life-threatening situation.

And finally, I've learned that it is so important to say thank you, again and again and again.

Reflection number 29

WE REAP WHAT WE SOW

'Doctor Benjamin Spock said that we shouldn't spank our children when they misbehave because their little personalities might get warped and we might damage their self-esteem.' And we said, 'Well, an expert should know what he's talking about, so we won't spank them anymore!'

Someone important said that teachers and principals should not discipline our children when they misbehave. The school administrators agreed and said, 'We didn't want any bad publicity concerning this subject, and we surely don't want to be sued.' We accepted their reasoning!

Someone said, let's let our daughters have abortions if they want, and they won't even have to tell their parents. And we said, 'That's a grand idea!'

A very wise man said, 'Since boys will be boys, and they're going to do it anyway, let's give our sons all the condoms they want, so that they can have all the fun they desire.' And we said, 'That's another grand idea!'

Someone said, 'Let's print magazines with pictures of nude women and call it wholesome down to earth appreciation for the beauty of the female body.' And we said, 'We have no problem with that!'

Someone else took that appreciation step further and published pictures of children, and then stepped even further by making them available on the Internet.

The entertainment industry said, 'Let's make TV shows and movies that promote profanity, violence and illicit sex. And let's record music that encourages rape, drugs, murder, suicide and satanic themes. And we said,

'It's just entertainment, it has no adverse effect, and nobody takes it seriously anyway, so go right on ahead!'

And now we're asking ourselves why our children have no conscience, why they don't know right from wrong, and why it doesn't bother them to kill strangers and even their classmates? Probably if we think about it long and hard enough, we can figure it out. It has a great deal to do with, 'WE REAP WHAT WE SOW.'

After a shooting at a school in America someone pinned a card on a bunch of flowers and left them attached to the school railings. The card read, 'Dear God; why didn't you save them?' Sincerely, concerned student.

The next day someone pinned a note beside it that read, 'Dear concerned student: I'm not allowed into your lives and into your schools.' Sincerely, God.'

If you agree with this reflection—fine! If you don't agree—fine! But don't ignore it and sit back complaining about what bad shape the world is in!

Reflection number 30

GOD BLESS OUR SENIOR CITIZENS

Old people are so special! We should always value them. They have so much experience and we could all learn so much from them if we would only take the time to sit down with them and listen. One of the lovely wee ladies that I call to on the first Friday of the month gave me this reflection. It's typical of our senior citizens, full of wisdom and full of wit. Let's make sure that we give them all the respect and the love that they deserve!

'Did you know that we old folks are worth a fortune? We have silver in our hair, gold in our teeth, stones in our kidneys, lead in our feet and gas in our stomachs. I am a frivolous old woman! Life is for living and I'm living mine to the full. At present I'm seeing a few men every day. Well, I've always enjoyed their company! As soon as I wake up every morning Will Power helps me out of bed and then I go to see Jimmy Riddle. After that it's time for breakfast with Mr. Kellogg, followed closely by the refreshing company of Mr. Tetley or my other friend who I know only by the initials of P.G. Then comes someone I don't like at all—Arthur Itis—he knows I'm not happy at him calling, but insists on being here, and what's more, he stays for the whole day. Even though he knows he's not welcome he annoys me all the more by moving all about the place, he takes me from joint to joint.

After a busy day I tell you I'm glad to get to bed (and with Johnny Walker too)—what a hectic life I lead! Oh yes, I admit it, I'm also flirting with Al Zheimer!

The priest called the other day and said at my age I should give some thought to 'The Hereafter'. So, I told him straight, 'Father, I think about 'The Hereafter' all the time, for no matter where I am, the bedroom, the kitchen, the living room or the garden, I ask myself—now what am I here after?' I hope that Will Power is your constant companion too. A word of advice, make sure that Emma Royd does not creep up on you from behind, and watch out for that old crafty one Gerry Atric—I'm wise for those two!'

Reflection number 31

KIND WORDS AND KIND DEEDS

In his first year at school, Tommy's teacher, Miss Grant, asked the children to draw a picture of a tepee. As she went around the class to look at their work, Miss Grant pointed out that Tommy's purple tepee wasn't realistic enough, that purple was the colour of people when they died, and that Tommy's drawing wasn't good enough to hang up on the wall with all the others. Tommy sat in his seat with his head bowed low, and with a black crayon Tommy brought nightfall to his purple tent in the middle of the afternoon.

In his second year Miss Rice invited the children to draw anything they wanted. Tommy left his paper blank for fear of his feelings being hurt again, and when the teacher came around to his desk, his tiny heart beat like a tom-tom. Miss Rice touched his red curly hair with her soft gentle hand, and in her kind voice she said, 'Beautiful Tommy! The snowfall! How clean and white and striking!'

Everyone needs affirmation and encouragement in life. It helps us grow, it gives us confidence and it makes us feel good about ourselves. A few kind words can so easily bring a smile to the face of babies, adults and senior citizens. We never really know how people are feeling when we meet them in the supermarket, in Church, or even if we're out walking. So many people are great actors and actresses, they can give Oscar performances pretending that everything is fine, while deep down they are broken and in pain.

That's why it's so important to be nice, to speak kindly, to ask people how they are, to listen, to smile and to offer help—it doesn't cost much, and yet it means so much.

A woman was standing at a pelican crossing waiting on the lights to turn green so that she could walk across. As she waited, she noticed a young girl of about seventeen at the other side who was also waiting for the green light. What drew her attention to the girl was the fact that she seemed upset, in fact she was crying. The woman kept her gaze on the young girl as they approached each other in the middle of the road. Everything in her wanted to reach out, to touch her, to reassure her that she cared, that nothing was beyond redemption and that she wanted to help. She hesitated, went back from her heart up to her head, and she met and passed the girl without any communication.

For a long time the woman was haunted by the look of pain on the girl's face, but most of all she was haunted by the fact that she did nothing to help.

Reflection number 32

COULD THE PROBLEM BE WITH ME?

A woman went into a supermarket, paid for her groceries and then headed into the nearby Coffee Dock that was within the shopping complex. She purchased a cup of coffee and a Kit-Kat bar and sat down at a table where a man was having a cup of tea. The woman nodded at him, put the bag of groceries beside her on the floor and began to sip her coffee.

The man sitting across from her immediately started to open the Kit-Kat bar. When he had finished taking off the silver wrapping paper he snapped it in two and began to eat the first piece. While chewing the Kit-Kat he smiled across at the woman who was really annoyed. The woman grabbed the remains of the chocolate bar from him, ate it angrily and said nothing.

The man got up, took his tea with him, purchased a jam doughnut from the counter and sat down at another table that was free.

This was all too much for the woman, and so she picked up her bag of groceries and as she was passing by his table on her way out, she lifted his doughnut and took a single bite out of it.

As the woman was putting the groceries into the back of her car, she found there, on the top of her groceries, in her shopping bag, her bar of Kit-Kat.

There are so many people in our society who are never wrong. They know absolutely everything and they are authorities on every subject under the sun. They are never prepared to listen or to see anyone else's point of view.

It's important to try and listen to those around us, and to ask ourselves from time to time could we possibly be reading a situation incorrectly? If we try, we could so easily avoid making total fools of ourselves!

One day as a woman was driving around a hairpin bend, she swung her car wide and forced a man who was coming in the opposite direction to swerve sharply in order to avoid a head on collision. To add insult to injury, or so it seemed, as the woman passed by the man, she cried out, 'Pig!' Hastily categorising the woman as an ignoramus, the man shouted back, 'Jackass!' And as he rounded the curve the man crashed his car straight into a huge pig that was standing right in the middle of the road!

Reflection number 33

PEACE AND GOODWILL

An elderly man found a magic lamp one day as he walked along the beach. He picked it up and a genie appeared before him. 'Because you have freed me,' the genie said, 'I will grant you a wish'.

The man thought for a moment and then responded. 'My brother and I had a fight some thirty years ago and he hasn't spoken to me since. I wish that he'll finally forgive me.' A huge sound of thunder could immediately be heard, and the genie proudly declared, 'Your wish has been granted.'

'You know' the genie continued, 'most men would have wished for wealth or fame, but you have only asked for the love of your brother. Is it because you are old or dying?' 'No way!' the man cried. 'But my brother is, and he's worth £60 million.

While it's nice at Christmas to send cards to friends, family and neighbours, lets take time to remember all those people that we do not speak to any more—all those who are not on our Christmas card list. When Mary and Joseph arrived in Bethlehem all they seemed to hear at each guesthouse was, 'No Room.' How many people are there around us that we close out, that we have no time and no room for anymore? How many people are there in our family that we are not prepared to let into our hearts? Let's not forget that the message of Christmas is one of peace and goodwill for 'all people.'

On Christmas morning some years ago, a little boy smiled as he tenderly handed over the Christmas present to his mother. Early on Christmas Eve he had shyly presented himself to a nice female shop assistant in town. 'I would like to buy my mother a new slip for Christmas,' he said bravely. 'Very nice,' the shop assistant replied, 'But first, I shall have to know more about your mother. Tell me; is she tall or small, heavy or thin?'

She's . . . eh . . . she's perfect,' the boy stammered. 'Perfect indeed,' the shop assistant laughed, and so she wrapped a slip that was size 34 for him. A few days later the mother returned the perfect 34 slip, and exchanged it for a size 52.'

If Christmas is to be truly 'perfect' for us, let's try and make peace with all that we have not been at peace with for some time now. In that way our hearts would be real stables!

Reflection number 34

ONE SOLITARY LIFE

It was the Christmas pageant at school. A young lad called Jimmy had been given a very simple job to do. Jimmy was the Inn Keeper. He had to stand at the side of the stage and tell Mary and Joseph that there was no room for them at his house. The whole class had rehearsed and practised the nativity play many times, but on the actual night when Mary and Joseph came along, Jimmy took them by the hand and welcomed them into his home with a big smile upon his face. Backstage afterwards Jimmy started to cry, because he knew that he was going to get scolded by the teacher for not doing what he was told. But in his wee heart and soul he just couldn't say that there was no room; because there was plenty. And, after all, Saint Joseph was his best friend in the playground!

He was born in an obscure village,
The child of a peasant woman.
He grew up in another obscure village,
Where he worked in a carpenter's shop until he was thirty.
Then for three years he was an itinerant preacher.
He never had a family or owned a home.
He never set foot inside a big city.
He never travelled two hundred miles
From the place he was born.
He never wrote a book, or held an office.
He did none of the things that accompany greatness.

While he was still a young man,
The tide of popular opinion turned against him.
His friends deserted him.
He was turned over to his enemies,

And went through the mockery of a trial.
He was nailed to a cross between two thieves.
While he was dying,
His executioners gambled for the only piece of
property he had—His coat.
When he was dead,
He was taken down and laid in a borrowed grave.

2000 years have come and gone, and today
Jesus is still the central figure for much of the human race.
All the armies that ever marched
And all the navies that ever sailed
And all the parliaments that ever sat
And all the kings and queens that ever reigned,
Put together,
Have not affected the life of any human being upon this earth
As powerfully as this "One Solitary Life."

Reflection number 35

THE CREED

I went to visit a friend of mine in hospital just before Christmas. He has been in hospital for such a long time, but he's certainly not giving up—he's a great guy! He gave me this helpful reflection when I called to visit him. It's for anyone who is finding life tough. He certainly finds life tough from time to time, but thank God he always keeps on trying.

Depression is a very common illness indeed, and yet sadly it is one that is still frequently misunderstood. It's important to remember that depression is not a sign of weakness, it is nothing to be ashamed of, and it can be treated successfully. The first step is just reaching out for help—just because life is tough, you don't have to be! Thank God for all those in the public eye who have been such inspirations to us by coming out on television and radio and telling their personal stories of living with depression.

My friend in hospital calls this reflection his 'Creed'—I hope that it may be of some help to someone who's reading this book today. It goes like this . . .

Your life is a journey ahead of you. Each day is a new beginning. Remember that yesterday is a friend who will guide you.

There will be good times and there will be bad times. Cherish the good times; because they make life sweet, but be thankful also for the bad times, for through them you will come to know the true meaning of life.

Naturally, there will come times when you face difficult decisions, and you won't know which way to turn. The most important thing is that you make a choice and that you move forward.

There will be times when you'll be unsure of what to believe in; believe in yourself, and you will never be without a direction.

There will be times that test your strength and endurance, but don't give up, refuse to accept defeat. Remember that perseverance is the key to success.

There will be times that you will be hurt by love. Forgive those who hurt you, so that your heart will be free to love again.

Naturally, there will be times when you make mistakes. Remember that mistakes are not a reflection of your self worth, but of your humanity.

There will be times when your search for happiness leads to frustration and disappointment. To be happy with the world you must first be happy with yourself.

There will be times when life seems unfair; there will be times when fear stands in the way of reaching out for your dreams. Confront your fears, and you will conquer them.

There will be times when your faith in God and your faith in humanity is shaken, but don't despair for it will return. Life gives everything that's needed to be happy; all you need to do is reach for it.

Reflection number 36

THE TOWN CRIER

Age is simply a quality of mind. If you have left your dreams behind, if hope is cold, if you no longer plan ahead, if ambitions are dead, then you are old.

But if you make of life the best, and in your life you still have zest, if love you hold, no matter how the years go by, no matter how the birthdays fly, you are not old.

On a street in San Francisco there is a funeral parlour with beige curtains covering the window. In front of the window there is a sign that reads, 'Why walk around half dead, when we can bury you for ninety eight dollars?'

Have you ever noticed that there are many people who are walking around half dead? They are not old, but they are without hope, without ambition, everything for them is a big effort.

Sometimes whenever I'm shopping and I see someone coming along who is going to start moaning and complaining, I slip into the nearest shop and pretend that I have to buy something.

There are so many people around who are not old, who are in full health, yet no matter when you meet them they have something to complain about—if it's not their ingrown toe nails, it's their pet labrador experiencing hot flushes and displaying early signs of menopause. They have absolutely no joy in their lives!

It's good to ask ourselves the following question:—In the morning whenever the alarm clock goes off, do we say: Good morning God? Or Good God, it's morning!

Wilma Rudolph was thought to be a disaster from birth. She was a tiny premature baby, who caught pneumonia, then scarlet fever and finally polio. *The polio left one of her legs badly crippled, with her foot twisted inwards. Until the age of eleven she hobbled around on a metal brace.*

Wilma asked her sister to keep watch every day while she tried to walk without her braces. She practiced for a very long time and was afraid that her parents might find out. Eventually, feeling guilty she told her doctor, who was flabbergasted. However, he gave her permission to continue as she was, but only for a short period of time.

Eventually Wilma threw her crutches away for good. She progressed to running, and when she was sixteen she won a bronze medal in the relay race at the Melbourne Olympics. Four years later at the Olympics in Rome, Wilma became the first woman in history to win three gold medals in track and field.

Wilma returned to a huge welcome in the US and received the Sullivan Award as the nations' top athlete—not bad for someone who was thought to be a disaster from birth!

Still feel like complaining?

Reflection number 37

REAL LOVE

Two warring tribes lived in the Andes, one in the lowlands and the other high up in the mountains. The mountain people invaded the lowlands late one night while everyone slept, and on top of all the plundering and destroying, they kidnapped a newborn baby.

The people from the lowlands didn't know how to climb the mountain; they didn't know any of the trails that the mountain people used, and they didn't know where to find them or how to track them in the steep terrain. Even so, they sent out their strongest party of fighting men to climb the mountain and bring the baby back.

The men tried first one method of climbing, then another and then another. However, after several days of effort they had only been able to climb several hundred feet. Feeling both hopeless and helpless the men decided that the cause was lost, and they prepared to return to their village below.

As they were packing their gear for the descent, they noticed in the distance a woman coming down from the mountain towards them. It was the baby's mother. She was coming down the very mountain that they hadn't figured out how to climb. And what's more, as she approached them, they could see that she had a baby strapped to her back.

One of the men greeted the young woman and said, 'We couldn't climb this mountain. How did you manage, when we, the strongest and most able men in the village couldn't?'

The woman calmly replied, 'It wasn't your baby!'

The two greatest commandments in the gospel are to love God and love our neighbour. Loving our neighbour can sometimes be very difficult indeed, but then who ever told us that loving someone was going to be easy?

Our neighbour takes on many forms. It can be the mother in law, the spoilt child next door, the boss at work, the brother's wife, the family member who's sick, as well as the poor person living in the darkest part of Africa.

How often do we not want to get involved because it's too much effort? How often do we say to ourselves, 'This is none of my business!' How often do we try to ease our conscience by slipping a few pounds to Oxfam or Concern and we think that we're doing something out of the ordinary?

Let's face it, our neighbours are all around us, and caring for them, which we're all called to do, may mean making more of an effort than we are at present.

If we really want to love our neighbour, we might try to stop saying, 'This is not my problem,' and begin saying, 'Can I offer any help here?'

Reflection number 38

THE LORD IS MY SHEPHERD

On a warm sunny afternoon a group of workmen began to discuss good and bad memories. As a result of their discussion, a wager was set as to who could remember a poem or a prayer and recite it word for word. A young apprentice stood up and began to recite the 23rd psalm that he had learned some years before at school. As everyone listened they realised that he had obviously received training in drama, in breathing techniques and in diction. Such was his delivery of the prayer that he recited it a second and third time to thunderous applause.

The second man to take part was elderly and stooped, and at times it was even difficult to hear him speaking. As he stood in the corner he recited, 'The Lord is my shepherd, there is nothing I shall want. Fresh and green are the pastures where he gives me repose.' When he had finished there was total silence as each man bowed his head and began to pray quietly to himself. The young apprentice came over to the old man and shook his hand. 'It is fairly obvious that I know the psalm' he said, 'but more obvious that you know the shepherd.'

How many of us really know Christ? How many of us really believe?

An evangelist was preaching to a large crowd of people who were gathered all around him. The evangelist pointed to a huge waterfall in the distance that had a tightrope going across it. He invited the crowd to follow him to the edge of the water and asked them, 'Do you believe that with God's help I can walk across this waterfall?' The crowd all cheered, 'We believe, we believe,' and as the evangelist walked across and back the people clapped and sang aloud, 'Praise God, praise God.'

The evangelist had two strong men pass him up a wheelbarrow which he balanced on the tightrope, and he shouted out to the crowd, 'Do you believe that with God's help I can walk across this waterfall wheeling this old barrow?' The crowd once again cheered, 'We believe, we believe,' and as he moved across the waters edge the people raised their hands in the air with great joy and they praised God at the top of their voices.

Finally, the evangelist asked the crowd, 'Do you believe that with God's help I can walk across this waterfall wheeling this old barrow with a person sitting inside of it?' The crowd became fanatical and they shouted repeatedly, 'We believe, Lord we believe!' The evangelist held his right hand in the air for silence and called out, 'Let the person who believes, jump in?'

For some strange reason there was no more cheering!

Reflection number 39

SAINT VALENTINE'S DAY

On Saint Valentine's Day I guess just about everyone will receive huge cards displaying rosy red hearts, apprentice cherubs practicing archery, and soppy sad verses inside with professions of starry-eyed and drippy love—well, everyone except Bart Simpson and me that is!

Valentine's Day is the day when we celebrate romantic love. Incidentally, it is also the day when card shops, post offices, florists, jewellers and restaurants celebrate. They celebrate because they make an absolute packet—and I'm not being cynical about the whole thing just because no one ever sends me a card or a red rose—honest to God, I'm not!

So, who was Saint Valentine and why do we celebrate this day? Some say that there were two different men named Valentine, the first was a Roman priest who was martyred during the persecution of Claudius around 269AD, and the second was a Bishop of Terni who was taken to Rome and martyred. Though the surviving accounts of both martyrdoms are legendry, it is just possible that both refer to the same person.

The nicest story I've come across about Saint Valentine is that he was imprisoned because he refused to worship pagan gods, and while in prison he made friends with the jailer's daughter who was cured of her illness because of his prayers. On the date of his execution (February 14th) the story goes that just before his death he sent her a note that was signed 'From Your Valentine'.

As Saint Valentine's Day is the feast of romantic love, let me tell you a heart-warming story about another kind of love.

There was once a large family who lived on a farm and who cared for their old frail grandmother. The doctor suggested that they might give her a small glass of brandy each night in order to help her digestion and her sleep. However, the old granny was a staunch pioneer and refused to take anything that would break her pledge.

The family loved Granny so much and they couldn't bear to watch her in any kind of discomfort, so, every night they would bring her a large glass of milk that was laced with Hennessey's finest Cognac.

For three years the old lady drank the mixture, and even licked her lips so as not to miss the last drop. Before she died, before she went to meet her God, she held her son's hand tightly and gently whispered into his ear, 'Whatever you do son, never ever sell that cow!'

Such a family would be richly rewarded by God, because each simple act of theirs was done to give comfort, joy, happiness and true love to their old granny.

Reflection number 40

ANYONE FOR SACKCLOTH AND ASHES?

My God—it's Lent again! It's only like yesterday that we were all running around like headless chickens frantically preparing for Christmas, and now I'm told that it's officially Spring and that Easter is just around the corner. Am I getting old or is time really flying?

For Christians, Lent is a journey towards Easter and the Resurrection of our Lord. Lent invites us to look closely at our lives, the way we live and the way we treat all those around us. It challenges us to make a change of heart where necessary—to become better people, kinder people, and more Christian people. It's also the time when many of us decide to cut back on food, sweets, cigarettes and alcohol—I strongly suspect that membership for Health Clubs, Unislim and Weight Watchers steadily increases during this particular church season, although not for any spiritual motive.

If you haven't yet decided what you're going to do for Lent, here's a wee story that might inspire you. Unfortunately, it'll not help you lose any weight like pounding the roads and giving up sticky buns might, but it may just help you become a better Christian.

One day a man went to Socrates. 'Hey, Socrates', he said, 'Have you heard what your good friend has done?

'Before you speak, interrupted Socrates, 'Have you put what you are going to tell me through the three sieves?'

'What do you mean by three sieves?' the man asked.

'It's a little check that we should all go through before we open our mouths,' explained Socrates. 'The first sieve is truth. So then, have you proof of everything you want to tell me?'

'No', the man said, 'I just heard a few people talking about it.'

'Well, have you tested it with the second sieve then? It's the sieve of goodness. If you can't prove that this information is true—is it at least something good?'

'Hesitantly the man replied, 'No, it's not. In fact it's the opposite.'

'Well,' said Socrates, 'Lets try the third sieve then, and ask ourselves whether its really necessary for you to tell me this information that you are so excited about?'

'Well,' said the man, 'If I'm honest, it's not really necessary that I tell this information to anyone'.

'Well then,' said Socrates smiling, 'if what you want to tell me is neither true, nor good, nor necessary, then forget all about it, and don't burden yourself or anyone else with it!'

We pray that when we open our mouths during Lent, and every day after that, our words will be truthful, good and necessary. And if they're not, we pray that we'll have a change of heart, and simply say nothing!

Reflection number 41

BILLY THE KID

It has often been said that Christianity suffers from an abundance of holy people and a great shortage of whole people. So often clergy lament that the media are out to constantly criticise and condemn them. Can the media help reporting what is sitting in front of their very eyes? Should we be surprised that young people find double standards repulsive?

During his lifetime Jesus furnished his followers richly with miracles, teachings and with great works of charity—he practiced exactly what he preached, and he demands both prayer and good works from all of us—not one, but both!

Perhaps this story might inspire us—it tells us that Christianity is of no use, unless it is lived.

Billy was a wild man in his youth! He sported huge shaggy red hair and wore washed out jeans with a tee shirt that had massive gaping holes in it. Billy walked around in his bare feet most of the time, he was highly intelligent, very unconventional and tremendous fun to be with—everyone loved Billy. During his time at college Billy became a Christian.

Across the road from the main campus was an extremely conservative Church, and one day Billy decided to visit. He walked in when the Service was just about to begin, and not seeing any seats available he made his way up the middle aisle and squatted down on the carpet, which was just beneath the pulpit. Although squatting on the floor was perfectly acceptable behaviour at college parties, it was not quite the norm in Church—especially this Church!

The Minister came out on to the sanctuary, welcomed everyone and invited them to join in singing the opening hymn as the procession made its way up from the back of the Church. An old man of eighty who was a

Church elder carried up the book of gospels in procession. The congregation watched with great anticipation to see what his reaction would be to this hippy-like creature squatting on the carpet. The Minister began to feel under great pressure, and wondered if steam was starting to rise from beneath his collar?

To everyone's amazement when the old man reached the top of the Church he simply put the book of the gospels into the pulpit and made his way to where Billy was. With great difficulty he lowered himself down on to the carpet beside Billy, smiled, and shook hands with him.

When the Minister's blood pressure finally settled down he said to the congregation, 'What I'm about to preach to you, you will never remember! What you have just seen, you will never forget. Be very careful every day how you live your lives, because you may just be the only bible that some people will ever read!'

Reflection number 42

HAPPY MOTHER'S DAY

There are four phrases that mothers never seem to hear—Well, all the mothers that I have ever met. Let me share them with you.

1. *'Mum, if you don't mind, I'd really like to contribute more money towards the housekeeping each week'.*
2. *'Instead of me going on a foreign holiday this year Mum and spending all of my money on outlandish clothes, I've bought you a new dishwasher—no arguing, I insist!'*
3. *'Mum—Is there anything I can do to help you?'*
4. *'Tell me what you think I should do Mum? I really value your advice!'*

Irish mothers are no fools—It'll take more than a funny card and a box of chocolates from the corner shop to show them that you care. Of course they'll smile and thank you profusely, but if you look closely into those big eyes, you might just see the sadness and the disappointment.

When it comes to our mothers, it's amazing how a little thing like calling out home for five minutes after work can mean so much, and how a big thing like a huge cheque inside a shop bought card can mean so little. Perhaps it's because when we call out home it says that we have time, and that we care, and when we send a cheque or a money voucher inside a card it says that we couldn't even make the time to get to the shop.

Irish parishes, in many ways, are a bit like the soap opera 'Dallas'—don't you think? Remember how every so often a new son or daughter would just appear out of nowhere? Where had they suddenly come from? Where had they been for the previous four years and two thousand episodes? However, in true soap opera style the story unfolded that a wicked witch had kidnapped them at birth and taken them off to the soapy land of 'Oz', and now, as if by magic, they were back home, re-united with all their loved ones.

It's amazing how at the death of an old person sons and daughters suddenly appear out of nowhere. Where had they been all those years when poor old Johnny and little old Molly were telling me that no one ever came to visit? Where were they all that time when S.V.D.P. was calling with food parcels and bags of coal?

Mother's day I suspect was invented by some card conglomerate as a means to making mega bucks—unfortunately, we can't do anything about that. But we can do something to put our child-parent relationships back on track, if they're not all they should be. Nobody, and least of all mothers should be left to end their day alone, deprived of the one thing that makes sense in their lives—their children!

Reflection number 43

PATRICK THE SAINT

From what I remember at primary school, I think Patrick was born in Scotland around 385. As children our teacher painted us a very sad story of how poor Patrick was captured by pirates and taken off to a land of Druids and pagans, and how as a slave he spent his time caring for sheep. Our class was happily relieved to hear that after many prayers, dreams and lengthy journeys Patrick managed to make it back home to his family and friends.

However, following his ordination Patrick returned to Ireland once more—this time to convert the very people who had captured him. Even as a child I couldn't help thinking, 'Is this guy a saint or what?'

Without wishing to shatter anyone's illusions, I'm afraid to profess it's an old myth that Patrick drove the snakes out of Ireland. On top of that we don't really know for sure that he used shamrock to explain to pagans about the Trinity.

Nevertheless, we do know that he converted thousands to Christianity (*although I'm told he wasn't the first person to preach the Christian message to the Irish—there were others before him*), and obviously he was a man who bore no ill will or hatred to those who had previously caused him such tremendous pain and heartache. His message then must have been one of love and forgiveness, as he certainly seems to have put those qualities into practice.

Saint Patrick's Day is certainly a day to be enjoyed—by all means eat, drink and be merry, but let's not forget that lovely message of love and forgiveness that we are all called to live every day.

Do you think if Patrick came back to Ireland now he might identify with this amusing story?

A new priest came to a country parish. He was young, handsome, exceptionally kind, and a wonderful preacher—his parishioners adored him.

On his first Sunday morning he preached a fabulous sermon all about love and forgiveness—it was the talk of the surrounding area. The next Sunday the parish church was jam-packed. However, as everyone settled down to hear his lovely words of wisdom, the priest set about preaching the very same sermon that he had given the previous week. No one said anything afterwards, in fact, even though they had heard it all before, he was lovely to look at just the same!

But, on the following Sunday when he repeated the same sermon for a third time, a few old women went around to the sacristy afterwards to talk to him. 'Father', they said, 'We just love your sermon'.

'Great', said the young priest, 'I'm delighted to hear that'.

'But we were wondering', they said, 'Have you any other sermons?'

'I have indeed', the priest said.

'Do you think we might hear them sometime?' an old dear piped up, 'We're all terribly eager to hear what you have to say—we find it all so challenging!'

'Ach surely' said the young priest, 'I'd be delighted to preach a different sermon. It's just that I've been watching very closely and I haven't seen you doing anything about that first one yet!'

Reflection number 44

LEARNING LESSONS THE HARD WAY

It must be hard as a parent to have to stand by and watch your children make their own mistakes. If they had just listened to your advice, all this unnecessary pain could so easily have been avoided. But then, in all honesty, how many of us were interested in listening to our parents' advice when we were growing up? How many of us thought we knew it all? How many of us only cared about enjoying ourselves?

I came across a great poster one day in Belfast. It read—*'Calling all young people—tired of your stupid parents always complaining? Why not move out, eat what you want, wash your own clothes, pay for everything yourself and clean up your own mess?'*

Lessons learned the hard way are somehow never forgotten. A friend of mine sent me this story—I think it's a cracker!

According to a news report, a Private Girls School in Victoria was faced with a unique problem—a number of the young ladies who attended the school insisted on applying make-up and lipstick in the school bathrooms each morning before classes began. While this seems pretty normal and harmless behaviour, the same young ladies took their behaviour one step further by pressing their luscious lips firmly against the mirrors, covering the surfaces with countless red, cherry and cerise prints.

Every evening the Caretaker would tirelessly remove the many lip prints; only to have the same girls smudge them back the very next day. The Principal decided that something radical had to be done to solve this problem once and for all. She summoned girls from each class to a meeting in one of the bathrooms. After a firm oration entitled 'Cleanliness is next to Godliness', the Principal pointed out to all present that the endless lip prints were causing a major problem for the poor Caretaker who was left to clean them off every day.

To demonstrate just how time consuming and how very difficult all this was, she asked the Caretaker to begin the cleaning process. Without delay the caretaker took an old mop from the cupboard, dipped it in the toilet bowl, and began washing all the mirrors. Since that day there have never been any lip prints left on the mirrors in that school!

There are Teachers, and then there are Educators!

Reflection number 45

GOD'S SPECIAL CHILDREN

While I love Christmas and all the merriment that surrounds it, I have to profess that I adore Holy Week and Easter—it's so sacred and special, with themes of service, suffering, death, resurrection, hope, life, light and love all woven through it.

For me this year the most moving Easter liturgy was without a doubt in our local Special School. The pupils there treated us to a sequence of live gospel stories, beginning with Jesus riding into Jerusalem on a donkey while the children waved palm branches.

When the story of the resurrection unfolded a very excited and nimble Jesus sprang from the tomb and ran among the crowds shaking hands and dispersing blessings to all and sundry. We were under no illusions—Jesus had definitely come back to life. Full of joy he radiated life and light, which of course is what the resurrection is all about.

To assist with the raffle the staff carried in two tables that were laden with chocolate eggs. The first table had large eggs wrapped up in pretty baskets with colourful bows, while the second table had small eggs in paper boxes. As the winners' names were announced I noticed that the children from this school didn't automatically go for the biggest or the most expensive egg—they were happy just to choose the one that was nearest to them.

Special children are not price tag conscious; they don't think as we think, they don't want as we want, their love is not conditional, they will hold the hand of anyone kind enough to offer it and they are created with smiles that can sometimes make us cry.

I hope you enjoy this touching story. *A teacher in a Special School began his religion class by saying to the children: 'Today I want to tell you about someone you all must meet. He's a person who loves you and cares for you.*

He's kinder than the kindest person you know. He's a person who forgives you whenever you do wrong. No matter what path you follow he is always ready to accept you, to love you and to understand.'

As he described Jesus the teacher noticed a small boy waving his arms around frantically and getting very excited. Not able to hold his delight at knowing the answer the child blurted out, 'I know the man you're talking about. He lives on our street.'

Special children don't always give us the exact answers we're looking for. They might not go to college or university, but they can always recognise love and goodness, and they can see Christ in anyone who is kind to them. What a pity we can't be more like them!

Reflection number 46

SEIZE THE MOMENT

Enjoy the reflection. Hopefully it might make you stop, think and make some changes.

I have a friend who lives by a three-word philosophy: 'Seize The Moment.' When I look around me she may just be the wisest person on this planet.

A while back I got to thinking about all those poor women on the Titanic who skipped their dessert on that fateful night in an effort to cut back and lose some weight. From then on I tried to be a little more flexible. How many women, celebrating their birthday, will eat at home because their husband didn't suggest going out to dinner until after the food had been prepared? Does the word refrigeration mean nothing to you? How often have your children wanted to talk to you, but instead they had to sit in silence while you watched a family crisis on a soap opera?

I cannot count the times I called my friend and said, 'How about going out to lunch in half an hour?' She would gasp and stammer, 'I can't I have clothes drying on the line or my hair is dirty or I wish I had known yesterday or I had a late breakfast and it looks like rain.' She died a few years ago. We never did get around to having lunch together.

Because we cram so much into our lives every day, we tend now to schedule our very headaches. We live on a sparse diet of promises that we make to ourselves when all our conditions are perfect. For example, we'll go back and visit our grandparents when our child is toilet trained. We'll entertain when we replace the living room carpet. We'll go on that second honeymoon when the children finish off at college.

Life has a way of accelerating, as we get older. The days get shorter and the list of promises to ourselves gets longer.

One morning when I woke up, I realised that all I had to show for my life was a litany of 'I plan to . . . I'm going to . . . and someday when things are settled down a bit I'll . . .'

Until Sunday past, my lips hadn't touched ice cream for two years. It's not that I was allergic to it, it's just that I figured out I might as well apply it to my tummy with a trowel and eliminate the digestive process. The other day I stopped the car and treated myself to a triple scoop. I can now say in all honesty that if my car had hit an iceberg on the way home, I would have died a happy person. Make sure that you do something every day that you want to, not something you should do.

A few questions: If you were going to die soon and had only one phone call you could make, who would you call and what would you say? When you ask someone 'How are you?'—do you hear their reply? When the day is over, do you lie in your bed and relax, or do hundreds of silly chores run through your mind? Ever lost touch with a really good friend because you were too busy?

Please remember: Life is not a race. Take it slower—hear the music before the song is all over.

Reflection number 47

THE SAMARITAN

One day when I was a first year in high school, I met a guy from my class walking home from school—his name was Kyle. It looked like he was carrying all of his books. I thought to myself, "Why would anyone bring home all their books on a Friday? He must really be a nerd."

As I was walking a bunch of older guys ran towards him. They knocked his books out of his arms and tripped him so that he landed in the mud. As his glasses went flying I saw them land in the grass about ten feet from him. As he looked up I could see terrible sadness in his eyes. My heart went out to him. So, I jogged over to him and as he crawled looking for his glasses I saw a tear in his eye. As I handed him his glasses, I said, "Those guys are jerks. They really should get lives." He smiled at me and said, "Thanks!" It was one of those smiles that showed real gratitude.

As I helped him pick up his books I asked him where he lived. As it turned out, he lived near me. He said that he had gone to private school. We talked all the way home, and I carried some of his books. He turned out to be a pretty cool guy. I asked him if he wanted to play a little football with my friends. He said yes. We hung out all weekend and the more I got to know Kyle the more I liked him, and my friends thought the same of him.

Monday morning came and on the way to school there was Kyle with the huge stack of books again. I stopped him and said, "Boy, you are gonna really build some serious muscles carrying these books everyday!" He laughed and gave me half of them. Over the next four years we became best friends.

Kyle was our class senior and had to prepare a speech for graduation day. He looked great. He was one of those guys that really 'found' himself during High School. He had more dates than I had, and all the girls loved him. Boy, sometimes I was jealous. I could see that he was nervous about his speech. So, I smacked him on the back and said, "Hey, big guy, you'll be great!" He looked at me with one of those looks (the really grateful one) and smiled. "Thanks," he said.

As he started his speech, he cleared his throat, and began, "Graduation is a time to thank those who helped you make it through those tough years. Your parents, your teachers, your siblings, maybe a coach . . . . but mostly your friends. I am here to tell all of you that being a friend to someone is the best gift you can give them. I am going to tell you a story".

I looked at my friend with disbelief as Kyle told the story of the first day we met. He had planned to kill himself over the weekend. He talked of how he had cleaned out his locker and was carrying all his books home. He looked hard at me and gave a smile. "Thankfully, I was saved. My friend saved me from doing the unspeakable."

I heard the gasp go through the crowd as this handsome, popular boy told us all about his weakest moment. I saw his Mom and Dad looking at me and smiling that same grateful smile. Not until that moment did I realise its depth.

'Never underestimate the power of your actions. With one small gesture you can change a person's life, for better or for worse. God puts us all in each other's lives to impact one another in some way. Please—look out for God in the people you meet.'

Reflection number 48

I LOVE YOU LOVE—WHO DO YOU LOVE?

A friendly bishop visited a primary school one afternoon to chat with the children preparing for Confirmation. After hymn singing and reading stories from the bible, the bishop asked a little girl, 'What is Matrimony?' The child beamed a huge Pollyanna like smile and politely answered, 'A place where souls suffer for a time on account of their sins.'

The parish priest who was accompanying the bishop began to laugh and said to the child, 'No, no, Mary, that's Purgatory, not Matrimony.'

'Oh, let her alone,' said the bishop. 'From what I see looking around me every day she just might be right. And anyway, what do you and I know about it?'

Marriage can be hard—very hard. I'm the first to admit that I couldn't do it! I often look around me at what some of my friends endure every day, and yes, I use the word endure, and I think that many of them deserve the George Cross.

Celibacy is difficult—very difficult, but marriage isn't easy either. Some years ago I was preaching in Rostrevor about how our Church needed to look at the possibility of optional celibacy. Afterwards a very wise old woman came into the sacristy to chat with me. In my foolishness I actually thought that she was coming to congratulate me on my homily. Instead, she took me aside and whispered gently into my ear, 'If you don't mind me saying it to you Father, you have a very naive and romantic notion of marriage—let me put the record straight for you. You were talking to us about loneliness in the priesthood, I can assure you the loneliest people in the world are very often married people.'

So why then do people still get married every day?—some even for the second, third and fourth time. Is it insanity, or the overwhelming desire to look like a massive meringue in public? Or, is it just fear that that you might end up dying in your own bed all alone?

On the other hand could it be that true love makes you want to commit your life forever to that 'Mr or Miss Right?' Do some people mix up the two L's (love and lust), and start off on the wrong foot from the word 'go'? Or has it something to do with the fact that happiness, sadness, poverty, prosperity, sickness and health weigh gently upon you as long as you're with that special person?

Whatever the reasons are, whenever I talk with young couples preparing for marriage, and whenever I see that magic that exists between them as they talk about their feelings for each other, I can't help but feel even slightly jealous.

The following is an old recipe for happiness in marriage. Check if you need any of the ingredients to add some flavour to your relationship?

Take five ounces of patience, a pinch of hope, two handfuls of hard work, a packet of prudence, a few sprays of sympathy, a bowl of honesty, and a jar of laughter.

Season with common sense and simmer gently in a pan of daily contentment.

Why not try it?

Reflection number 49

OUR LOVE IS NOT TO BE JUST WORDS OR MERE TALK

Story number one—*A young wife called her husband on the telephone one morning at work. She could hardly catch her breath with excitement as she blurted out to him that she had just won the Lotto. 'Can you believe it?' She cried 'The Lotto!' Her husband Harry was over the moon, and began thinking of how they would start celebrating and spending their millions. 'Imagine—the Lotto,' she kept repeating over and over again, 'you must come home immediately and start packing your clothes.'*

'Summer clothes or winter clothes?' laughed Harry, as he began to think of luxurious holiday cruises and skiing trips. 'Why all of them', she replied curtly, 'I want you out of the house for lunch time!'

Story number two—*An old man in America was driving around a huge car park one day looking for a free space. Just as he found one a cheeky teenager in a flashy sports car whizzed past him and drove straight into it. The old man began to protest, but the teenager laughed and poked fun at the old man shouting, 'Face it granddad—I'm younger and I'm better looking!'*

In his anger the old man slipped his car into first gear and immediately set about ramming the flashy sports car again and again and again. The teenager sat there in total shock as he watched his babe magnet being smashed to smithereens.

When he was finished his frenzied attack the old man wound down the window of his car, smiled at the teenager and said, 'Face it sonny—I'm older, but I have much better insurance than you!'

When our so called Christianity is divorced from our everyday living and the way that we treat people—when we carry on like those in the stories, we are like a lamp that gives no light or salt that has lost it's taste—we are nothing more than phonies and hypocrites.

If in one breath we'd call ourselves Christians and in the next breath we'd sell our mother to make a few pounds, (and believe me, there are some who would do it) then we have a very strange understanding of what Christianity is, and what it calls all of us to do.

The singer Fergal Sharkey of The Undertones had a hit single out many years ago. The chorus went, 'A good heart these days is hard to find—true love the lasting kind.' Good hearts full of love and Christian values are often hard to come by these days. Many of us are able to talk the talk, but not quite as able to walk the real walk.

Saint John in his Letter states, 'My children, our love is not to be just words or mere talk, but something real and active.'

How active a Christian are you?

Reflection number 50

AN EXAMPLE OF LOVE

Josephine was only a little girl when her family moved to California. She was in the third grade at the local school, and every morning the bus would pick her up outside her home, just like it did all the other kids, and every afternoon it would drop her off again.

When she stepped off the bus, Josephine's brother was always waiting for her by the fence that surrounded their home. He was a year or so older than Josephine, but he didn't go to her school.

Some of the other children on the bus used to look for him, and when they saw him they would laugh. They laughed because somehow they recognised that he was different. He looked and he acted differently from the other kids. They didn't know why, and they didn't understand, so they laughed. They would wave to him and call out to him, and he in turn would wave back to them. However, this only made them laugh all the more.

When Josephine got off the bus her brother would jump up and run to meet her. And to the other children's surprise, Josephine didn't seem embarrassed at all; though she knew behind her some of the kids were having a great time. She would smile at her brother and hug him, and often she would just drop her books on the ground and throw both arms around him. And then, hand in hand, the two of them would march together into the house.

Josephine was only a little girl, but she had learned a very human lesson of love. And it took time, the rest of the school year in fact, for the other children to learn that lesson as well.

Obviously some of the childrens' parents had heard about their mocking behaviour, and had spoken to them about it. And then some of the more perceptive children felt that somehow it wasn't right to mock this child, and their example in turn affected some of the others. Therefore, they began to show a little kindness and compassion.

When anyone would ask Josephine about her brother, Josephine would simply say that her brother was 'special', and that he would never be like all the other kids, but he was her brother and she loved him.

Later on, a couple of the children from Josephine's school came over to play at her house, and when they met Jimmy, they played with him too.

The children on the bus would still wave at Jimmy, but this time it wasn't in mockery, it was with real gentleness and friendship, and he in turn would wave back at them.

Josephine travelled on the school bus for many years, until finally her family moved away. But the image of those daily visits of Josephine embracing her brother and the evolving reaction of those kids on the bus remained in the memories of those children for a long, long time. Otherwise you wouldn't have heard this story, which was given to me by a fifty-year-old woman who was one of those children.

Reflection number 51

A PRAYER FOR THE STRESSED

A friend of mine slipped me this witty prayer a few weeks ago—it's one that I can certainly relate to, although I imagine it's not one that I would care to pray out loud in Church.

> *'God, grant me the serenity to accept the things I cannot change, the courage to change the things I cannot accept, and the wisdom to hide the bodies of those I had to kill today because they just got on my nerves and drove me around the bend.*
>
> *Also, help me to be careful of the toes I step on today, as they may be connected to the feet I may have to kiss tomorrow.*
>
> *Help me always to give 100% at work—12% on Monday, 23% on Tuesday, 40% on Wednesday, 20% on Thursday and 5% on Friday.*
>
> *Help me to remember that when I am having a bad day and it seems that people are trying to wind me up, it takes 42 muscles to frown, 28 to smile, and only 4 to extend my arm and smack someone on the jaw!'*

It seems that almost everyone today is suffering from stress in one form or another. Young people are stressed because of study, the pressure of exams, having to endure an empty, pathetic social life, and by and large not being understood or affirmed enough by their parents, their teachers and the whole world in general.

Adults are stressed with everything from children that won't sleep at night, a boss at work whose second name must surely be 'Adolf', and a partner at home who wants them to earn more money, buy a bigger house and take them on at least four foreign holidays each year.

Whatever our situation, there's one thing for sure, if we're stressed, if we're constantly under pressure, if life always seems to be always working against us, then we're definitely doing something wrong. The 'smart person' in today's world will take the time to find out what is wrong, and will make permanent changes. The 'not so smart person' will just keep trodding on, and spend the rest of their days lurching from crisis to crisis, until of course a massive coronary ends it all.

I've always believed that Christ never meant any of us to be miserable, or to be unhappy, or to be stressed with life. If we are, I suspect that we may just be missing something momentous about his message.

Perhaps this passage from 'Matthew 6' might help us to sit down and realize just what is important, and what's not important in life. 'Then Jesus said to his disciples, "That is why I am telling you not to worry about your life and what you eat, nor about your body and how you are to clothe it. Surely life means more than food and the body more than clothing. Can any of you, for all your worrying, add one single cubit to the span of your life? If the smallest things then, are outside your control, why worry about the rest? Think of the flowers; they never have to spin or weave; yet I assure you, not even Solomon in all his regalia was robed like one of these. Now if that is how God clothes the grass in the field which is there today and thrown into the furnace tomorrow, will he not much more look after you, people of little faith?"'

Reflection number 52

WHOSE SIDE ARE YOU ON?

A fancy dress parade attracted many spectators to a local town. As angels, leprechauns, pop stars and astronauts paraded up and down the main street, the crowd roared and clapped with great excitement. Unfortunately, in the middle of all the great festivities the heavens suddenly opened and the rains flooded down. Everyone immediately ran for cover, and within seconds the streets were deserted.

In the chaos, an old man who had dressed up to look like Satan couldn't find his wife, and in order to get out of the rain quickly and avoid a nasty bout of influenza, he promptly headed for the nearest doorway, which just happened to be a side entrance to the Church hall.

Inside a prayer meeting was taking place, and as Satan walked through the doors sporting his roaring red attire; and armed with pitchfork, horns and long curly tail, the crowd screamed for their lives and immediately scurried for the exit, like rats deserting a sinking ship.

In the confusion a poor woman's coat got caught in her chair. Unable to escape she squealed and begged for someone to help, but sadly no one came to her aid. The old man sauntered towards her in all his regalia, and was about to explain that he was merely taking part in a fancy dress parade, when the woman begged and pleaded aloud with him, 'Satan, Satan, I know I went to Church every morning for the last twenty years, but honest, I really was on your side all that time!'

If we're honest, whose side are we on? Are we Christians or are we nothing more than a bunch of phonies or hypocrites? Do we see the Ten Commandments as Ten Commandments, or are they nothing more than ten suggestions that don't always fit in with our current plans?

When you think of it, no one seems to steal anymore, they simply lift something, no one seems to lie anymore, they simply misrepresent the facts, and no one seems to commit adultery anymore, they simply play around—we seem to be able to invent excuses for almost every situation under the sun, and if we want to, we can be selective about Christ and his teachings whenever it suits us.

Calling a spade an agricultural instrument does not change what it is, and no matter how we try to dress up some of our modern day trends (that are really not modern at all) and our underhand behaviour, it will never take away from the fact that what is wrong, is wrong!

Whose side are you on?

Reflection number 53

BUTCHERS AND BISHOPS

A local butcher had meat delivered to many of his customers on a Friday—his young apprentice was usually assigned the job.

One warm afternoon the young apprentice cycled up to the Archbishop's house, rang the doorbell and waited, expecting little old Margaret the housekeeper to answer. However, on this particular afternoon the Archbishop himself happened to be passing by the front hall and went to see who was at the door. The young apprentice got a fright when he saw the Archbishop. He was a haughty man who instilled fear rather than respect, and in a panic the young apprentice almost threw the parcel at him. 'There's the meat,' he said, and took to his heels.

'Wait,' said the Archbishop, 'That's not the way you address an Archbishop. Let me show you. You go inside, answer the door and act as if you're me. I will stand out here and act as if I'm you.'

Within a moment the doorbell rang, the young apprentice answered, and the Archbishop stood on the steps smiling. 'Good afternoon Archbishop,' he said, 'I have meat here for you that has been sent up from the butcher's shop. I hope you have a very pleasant weekend and a most enjoyable meal—God bless.'

The young apprentice stood in the large hallway, received the parcel of meat, smiled and said, 'Thank you.' And with that he took a few pounds out of his pocket and said, 'Here my son, have a wee treat on me this weekend, I remember what it was once like to be young!'

So often we complain about what's wrong with the world today. We rattle on about how times have changed, and not for the better, how no one has the time to stop and speak any more, and how young people have no respect—but we rarely stop to ask ourselves: 'Could the problem ever be with me? Is there anything here that I'm doing wrong?'

If we want the world to be a much better place than what it is at present, let's begin any changes that are needed with ourselves!

Reflection number 54

LET GO AND LET GOD

I have often thought that the world is full of drivers as opposed to motorists. Wives drive their husbands, who of course return the favour by driving them around the bend. Parents drive young children, as young children do their parents, though not always consciously. Pupils drive their teachers to near despair, and I have no doubt that some teenagers drive their parents to almost breaking point.

'Driving' implies coercion—all of which is intended for someone else's good. Sadly however, no good ever comes of it. How often have we noticed young people abandoning their faith because their parents were over zealous in passing it on to them.

We mightn't always like the way our family choose to live, or what they choose or rather don't choose to believe in, but it's so important 'to live and to let live'. If we truly believe in God and his healing power, let's bring our troubles to Him, but let's make sure that we leave them there with Him. Christ said, 'I am the Way,' and if we removed the obstacles of ourselves, many people might find that Way.

Hope you enjoy this sound advice. If you can, try to put it into practice?

'I am God. Today I will be handling all of your problems. Please remember that I do not need your help.

*If life happens to deliver a situation to you that you cannot handle, do not attempt to resolve it, kindly put in the **S.F.G.T.D.***

(something for God to do) box. All situations will be resolved, but in "My time, not yours."

Once the matter is placed into the box, do not hold onto it by worrying. Instead, focus on all the wonderful things that are present in your life now. For example, if you find yourself stuck in traffic, don't despair. There are people in this world for whom driving is a luxury they know they will just never be able to afford.

Should you have a bad day at work, think of the person who has been out of work for years.

Should you despair over a relationship gone bad, think of the person who has never known what it is like to love and be loved in return.

Should you grieve the passing of another weekend, think of the woman in dire straits, working twelve hours a day, seven days a week to feed her children.

Should your car break down leaving you miles away from assistance; think of the paraplegic who would love the opportunity to take that walk.

Should you notice a new grey hair in the mirror, think of the cancer patient in the middle of chemotherapy who wishes that he or she had hair to examine.

Should you find yourself at a loss and pondering what is life all about, asking what is the purpose of all this, be thankful. There are those who didn't live long enough to get such an opportunity.

Should you find yourself the victim of other people's bitterness, ignorance, smallness or insecurities, just remember, things could be worse—You could be one of them!

Reflection number 55

POOR MARGARET INDEED!

Margaret received a parrot for her birthday. Her family thought it would be good company for her, as Margaret was unmarried and lived alone. The parrot was fully grown with a very bad attitude and even worse vocabulary. Every other word was an expletive, and those that weren't expletives were at the very least, rude.

Margaret tried to change the bird's attitude by constantly saying polite words and playing soft music. However, nothing worked. Margaret ended up yelling at the bird—the bird got worse. She shook the cage—the bird got madder and even ruder.

Finally, in a moment of sheer desperation Margaret grabbed the parrot by the throat and put it in the freezer—it appeared that she just couldn't take the temper tantrums and crude language any longer. For a few moments she could still hear the bird swearing, squawking, kicking and screaming, and then suddenly there was absolute quiet.

Margaret became frightened that she might have actually hurt the bird and so she quickly opened the freezer door. The parrot calmly stepped out onto Margaret's extended arm and said, 'I'm sorry that I have offended you with my bad language and my exasperating behaviour. Please grant me your forgiveness Margaret. I will endeavour to correct my conduct from this moment on.'

Margaret was astounded at the bird's new attitude and was just about to ask what was the reason for this massive change that took place inside the freezer when the parrot continued, 'May I ask exactly what the frozen chicken did?'

In a strange and cruel way our Society has a habit of pitying women who don't marry (the modern-day Margarets of our time). We buy them ridiculous presents like talking parrots and fluffy poodles, and we make horrible comments behind their backs like, 'Such a pity poor Margaret never met someone, she would have made someone a great wife.' Notice that single men are never referred to as 'poor', or as 'good china left on the shelf'?

Anyhow, who knows, but maybe Margaret made a decision that she didn't want to marry. Perhaps she looked around at some of her friends who endure relationships day in and day out that can only be described as hell upon earth, and she made a very rational decision to remain single.

Could it be that Margaret just didn't meet Mr Right along the way, but instead met Mr Rude, Mr Crude, Mr Horrible, Mr Mean, Mr Nasty, Mr Violent and Mr Pathetic, and thus decided that single life was a much better option? Or on the other hand, possibly Margaret takes a good look at her brothers and sisters when they visit her on Sunday, and she feels sorry for them. Maybe Margaret sees that look in their eyes, that look that seems to say, 'Is this it? Is this all there is to my life?'

Let's remember that those who are single pay their own way in society, and they are not some sort of reject or second hand rose. Remember Martha and Mary in the gospel? They must have easily been in their thirties, and both they and their brother Lazarus were Christ's very special friends.

Whatever single people want out of life it's not pity from those who are married!

Reflection number 56

SLOW ME DOWN LORD

Life is such a rat race—we're all in one huge rush! Where we're all rushing to is a very good question indeed, perhaps one we might stop and ask ourselves sometime.

Let's be honest, how many of us haven't time to talk, haven't time to listen, haven't time to visit, haven't time to phone, and haven't time to pray? It would appear now that we're so busy with work commitments that we haven't even time for those we profess to love. I have a sneaking suspicion that all this rushing about helps us to create some sort of delusion of self-importance—how ridiculous are we?

Before your relationship ends in tears, before you take a massive coronary, before you spend a fortune on stress counselling, back massages and relaxation therapy, try reading the following reflection and remembering that whenever God made us, He meant us to be happy, not stressed out and miserable. And if you are feeling stressed out and miserable, remind yourself frequently, that you're definitely doing something wrong.

Slow me down Lord; ease the pounding of my heart by the quieting of my mind. Steady my hurried pace with a vision of the eternal reach of time.

Give me amid the confusion of the day, the calmness of the everlasting hills. Break the tensions of my nerves and muscles with the soothing music of the singing streams that live in my memory.

Help me to know the magical, restoring power of sleep. Teach me the art of taking one-minute breaks—of slowing down to look at a flower, to chat with a friend, to pat a dog, to read a few lines from a good book.

Remind me each day of the fable of the hare and the tortoise, that I may know that the race is not always to the swift, that there is more to life than increasing speed.

Let me look upwards into the branches of the towering oak, and know that it grew great and strong because it grew slowly and well.

Slow me down Lord, and inspire me to send my roots deep into the soil of my life's enduring values, that I may grow towards the stars of my greater destiny.

Reflection number 57

GETTING IT RIGHT

While chatting with little Mary one day on the main street, the subject came around to poor wee Alice who had died suddenly the previous week. I knew that while Mary was concerned about Alice, she was also being nosey and was trying her best to find out any information she could about how much money Alice might have left behind in her will. Realizing that I knew nothing about Alice's finances, the bold Mary threw one last question at me, in the hope that as she left me, she might go away with more news than when she met me. 'Father', she said, 'what did poor Alice die of'? Having had enough at this stage, I mustered up my most sympathetic face ever, and gently replied, 'Well to be honest Mary, I think she died of a Tuesday.'

So many people, both young and old, worry about silly unimportant things, and involve themselves in dilemmas that really are none of their concern. They are interested in matters that have nothing to do with them, while at the same time they neglect huge important issues that are their responsibility.

Hope you enjoy the following beatitudes—there's a lot we can all learn from them!

Blessed are those who can laugh at themselves: they will have no end of fun.
Blessed are those who can tell a mountain from a molehill: they will be saved a lot of bother.

Blessed are those who know how to relax without looking for excuses: they are on the way to becoming wise.

Blessed are those who know when to be quiet and listen: they will learn a lot of new things.

Blessed are those who are sane enough not to take themselves too seriously: they will be valued by all those around them.

Happy are you if you can take small things seriously and face serious things calmly: you will go far in life.

Happy are you if you can appreciate a smile and forget a frown: you will walk on the sunny side of the street.

Happy are you if you can be kind in understanding the attitudes of others: you may be taken for a fool, but this is the price of charity.

Happy are you if you know when to hold your tongue and at the same time smile: the Gospel has begun to seep into your heart.

Blessed are they who think before acting and pray before thinking: they will avoid many blunders.

Above all . . . . Blessed are those who recognise the Lord in all whom they meet: the light of truth shines in their lives and they have found true wisdom.

Reflection number 58

EQUALITY FOR ALL

A good friend of mine gave me this story—it reminded him so much of sad and painful days gone by. I think it's one that many of us might be able to identify with.

I passed my childhood in Ireland. In class three of the national school we had a very strict teacher. While he was in the class our teacher often had visits from other members of staff, from parents, and from different acquaintances. Before leaving the classroom to talk to his visitors, he always appointed his favourite pupil, Paddy, to be in charge of the class.

Paddy was a rather large, sturdy, red haired boy who sat in the back row. His task was to write names up on the blackboard of any boys or girls who talked or carried on while the teacher was out. Within seconds a whole list of names was written up, and it was then, that Paddy began his dealing.

One of his victims would beg for mercy. 'Rub my name out and I'll give you a sweet at break time.' 'No it must be at least three sweets.' 'The most I'll give is two.' 'Two's not enough.' 'All right then, three.'

Other victims gave apples, chocolates and even glass marbles. Real 'criminals' had to get out of it with a pocket-knife or even a water pistol.

When the dreaded teacher returned there were always three or four names still on the blackboard. These were the poor children who had no money and no goods to trade with, and so they could not buy their names off the blackboard. These same children regularly received a number of strokes of the cane. I remember that there were many tears shed in our classroom.

This was a shock for me. For the first time in my life I experienced how the rich are privileged. Of course it was certainly not the last time in life I was to experience this.

Realistically, money talks all languages. To quote old J.R. Ewing: 'absolutely everyone has their price, it just depends baby on how much yours is?' Deals behind backs have always been done and always will, favouritism has always been shown, people have always worked from the premise, 'you scratch my back and I'll scratch yours', and those who think this sort of thing doesn't happen, are naive and foolish.

Thankfully Christ doesn't think or work or operate like we do. He doesn't show favouritism, discrimination or give preferential treatment to anyone; and he's certainly not interested in what we have or what we haven't got.

Throughout the gospels we constantly see instances where Jesus healed all of the sick and where he fed everyone. He didn't ask how much money people had, he didn't ever want to know who people were living with and he didn't think when he was helping someone as to how he might work this situation to his advantage in the future. All he was interested in was showing real kindness and real love to everyone around.

Perhaps today we could try and make Christ's motto our motto. We could try and be fair, just like Christ was. We could try to be kind, just like Christ was, and we could try to show love, just like Christ did, not just to a particular or select group, but to everyone.

Reflection number 59

A LITTLE SOMETHING TO THINK ABOUT

Late one night a very serious meeting took place in hell. Daddy devil himself stood up in front of his workers and spoke eloquently about the colossal damage being done on earth by recent religious renewal programmes. He mentioned in detail Christian Family Movements, Charismatic Renewal, Medjugorje Prayer Groups, Boys Brigades and Parish Missions. As his employees listened, he shouted aloud that if all this 'Good Work' was allowed to continue, he would soon be handing out P45's. Everyone grabbed their tails in total shock as he invited suggestions from the floor for a plan that might help him turn this unacceptable situation around.

Within a moment or so, one little devil held up his pitchfork and said that he had an idea that might just do the trick. 'Why don't we just spread the word around that there really is no such place as hell,' he said, 'everyone will be delighted. They will tell themselves that they can do whatever they want, since they'll all be going to heaven anyway!'

Everyone cheered and applauded, 'The day has been saved,' they cried in unison, but Daddy devil who was older and wiser shook his head and stamped his feet angrily on the podium. 'No, no,' he said, 'you don't understand the human species, they would never believe that. You see, even when they are children, they know when they do something wrong, they even have that awful guilty look written across their faces. At times they believe that they are even punished by their sins. No, no, I'm afraid they would never be taken in by such a suggestion!"

Feeling very deflated the little devil sat down, while his master demanded more suggestions. Eventually, another devil stood up and announced to all and sundry what he thought was a very new and extremely bright idea. 'Suppose we tell them that there is a hell,' he cackled, 'but that there's no such place as heaven. Everyone will say to themselves, "What's the use in even trying to be good? We're all going to go to hell anyway."'

Despite the fact that everyone shouted approval, Daddy devil again dismissed this idea. 'You just do not understand the human species,' he said, 'they would never believe that. Human beings are born with some sort of resilience in them, even if today is lousy, they somehow expect that tomorrow will be better. I never can fully work it out, there is something inside them, something put there by God, that always gives them hope for a better tomorrow.' 'More suggestions devils, please?' As his entire workforce stood around contemplating redundancy, Daddy devil suddenly began to laugh. 'I have it,' he bellowed, 'I have it. Why did I not think of this before?' 'We'll tell everyone we meet that there is a heaven, and there is a hell, but most important of all, we'll tell them that there's no hurry!' Everyone screamed and cheered, and as the raised Daddy devil up on their shoulders he shouted aloud, 'We're back in business boys, we're back in business. The whole secret is to convince people to sit back and think that they have all the time in the world to change!'

Have you ever heard that comment being passed around?

Reflection number 60

GO CRAZY FOR CHRISTIANITY

It has often been said that too much religion is worse than too little. How many people today have given up the practice of their faith because their parents literally shoved it down their throats when they were children?

Hope you enjoy this story—*An old parish priest got fed up with his parishioners only coming to Church when it suited them. He felt that his duties were merely hatch, match and dispatch (i.e. baptisms, marriages and funerals), and that the people in his parish were nothing more than 'A la Carte Christians'. Something radical needed to be done, a massive shake up needed to take place, and so he invited a battalion of missioners to come and detonate some real religion in his parish. The locals got wind of what the parish priest was up to and decided unanimously that they were having none of it.*

On the opening night of the mission a massive beefy looking missioner burst out on to the sanctuary armed with black biretta, Olympic stopwatch and a face like a bucket full of piranhas. In the church sat one solitary man, a man who lived on his own up in the mountains, a man who hadn't visited the town for a long time, a man who was unaware that the locals were boycotting the 'Go Crazy For Christianity Week'.

As he looked around him the missioner was suddenly unsure of what he should do. Was it worth his while treating this one solitary punter to such an awe-inspiring sermon? However, when he asked the question as to whether or not he should bother preaching, his lone disciple earnestly replied, 'Well Father, I'm just a simple man. I live on my own away up in the mountains, and I start off each morning by feeding my hens—I have thirty hens in total. However, if I call them for their breakfast Father, and only one hen comes out, I make sure that I feed that one, even if all the rest are not hungry.'

The missioner got the message loud and clear, and immediately began his homily with a huge tirade about the lust and the licentiousness that exists in the world today. Drawing to a halt some hours later he leaned over his pulpit and questioned the wee mountain man, 'Now, tell me, what did you think of that for a sermon?'

The man looked blandly up into the missioner's eyes and wearily responded, 'Well Father, as I said I'm just a simple man. I live on my own away up in the mountains, and I start off each morning by feeding my hens—I have thirty hens in total. However, if I call them for their breakfast and only one hen comes out, while I make sure Father that I feed that one hen, I sure as hell don't give her the whole bucket of meal!'

Religious convictions are always best served gently, quietly and with great understanding and Christ-like compassion for those around us!

Reflection number 61

THE POWER OF HOLDING HANDS

A wee toddler wandered out through an open door, and made his way into the cold, dark, wet and dirty night. He was gone for only a few minutes before his mother missed him. She called out his name but heard no answer. She tried the basement and the bedrooms upstairs; but he was nowhere to be found.

In sheer desperation she ran to the farmyard nearby where all the local workmen were finishing up, but he hadn't gone there either. As it happened there were huge wheat fields for miles in all directions. A search party organised itself almost immediately, but it bore no fruit on that wet, miserable night.

At dawn the next morning everyone gathered in force again, searching frantically for the poor wee boy. Eventually an old man called the group of helpers together. 'This is crazy' he said. 'We're going every way to find this child, everyway but the right way. He might be only two or three yards away from us in the tall wheat, and we wouldn't notice him. Why don't we all line up, hold hands, move together in the same direction, and comb the area, inch by inch?'

So, they held hands together, and began to walk through the first field. After moving only thirty yards they found the child—he was lying motionless in a gully.

They placed the little boy in his mother's arms while she sat on the doorstep with people looking on. And as the tears streamed down her face, she screamed from somewhere within the depths of her soul, 'In God's name, why didn't you people hold hands sooner?'

If family members could only hold hands together and let go of all the pettiness that so ridiculously divides them, imagine the love that might be shared.

Reflection number 62

A BETTER WORLD?

The paradox of our time in history is that we have taller buildings but shorter tempers; wider motorways, but narrower viewpoints.

We spend more but have less; we buy more, but enjoy it less.

We have bigger houses and smaller families; more conveniences, but less time; we have more degrees, but less sense; more knowledge, but less judgement; more experts, but more problems; more medicine, but less health.

We drink too much, smoke too much, spend too recklessly, laugh too little, drive too fast, get too angry too quickly, stay up too late, get up too tired, read too seldom, watch T.V. too much and pray too seldom. We have multiplied our possessions, but reduced our values. We talk too much, love too seldom, and hate too often.

We've learned how to make a living, but not a life; we've added years to life, not life to years. We've been all the way to the moon and back, but we have trouble crossing the street to say hello to our neighbour.

We've conquered outer space, but not inner space. We've done larger things but not better things. We've cleaned up the air, but polluted the soul. We've split the atom, but not our prejudice. We write more, but learn less. We plan more, but accomplish less. We've learned to rush, but not to wait. We build computers to hold more information to produce more copies than ever, but we have less communication.

These are the times of the fast food and slow digestion; tall people, and short character; steep profits, and shallow relationships. These are the times of world peace, but domestic warfare; more leisure, but less fun; more kinds of food, but less nutrition.

These are the days of two incomes, but more divorce; of fancier houses, but broken homes. These are the days of quick trips, disposable nappies, throwaway morality, one night stands, overweight bodies, and pills that *can do everything from cheer you up to relax you and kill you. It is a time when there is much in the shop window and nothing in the stockroom; a time when computer technology can bring this exact piece of information to you, and a time when you can choose either to share this insight, or perhaps just hit the delete button.*

Certainly interesting all right! Can you see yourself in any of the above? However, what's more important, can you really be bothered to make any changes?

Reflection number 63

THE FAMILY SERVANT

Honestly, how many of us take our parents or our spouse totally for granted, and just expect them to be there at our beck and call for all time?

I remember in a previous parish where I worked, a mother of a grown up family decided one day that she had enough, and so she packed her bags, walked away from the family home, and never came back. I met one of her grown up sons a week or so later, and out of courtesy I asked him how he was, and how things were going at home? When he told me that he and his brothers and sisters missed their mother desperately, I couldn't stop myself from answering, 'Well, I can certainly understand how you're feeling. If I had a servant who attended to my every need, every minute of my every day, I would miss her too if she left.'

Unfortunately for many of us, it's only when we are inconvenienced or left to fend for ourselves, that the penny drops and we begin to realise how totally spoiled we actually are. Many of us have got so used to having servants around us, that we just expect to be waited on hand and foot every day. How many people, young and old, don't know how to say the word 'thank-you'?

Does this story speak to you? *A young husband and father arrived home from work one evening to find his three children dressed in their pyjamas and playing out on the lawn. The curtains throughout the house hadn't yet been drawn, and every single room looked like it had been hit by a bomb. Games, food, dirty dishes and dirty washing were strewn all over the landing, stairs and the kitchen. Televisions, stereos and radios blasted together throughout the house, and every floor was messy and smelly where food had been walked into the carpets. Frantically fighting his way up the stairs amid what seemed like thousands of toys, the young man ran into the bedroom to check if his wife was alive or dead.*

To his great surprise his lovely wife was lying there in bed flicking through the pages of the latest copy of 'Hello Magazine.' When he roared 'What the hell's going on here?' His wife calmly replied, 'Well honey it's like this. You know every evening when you return home from work totally stressed out, and you sarcastically ask me what did I do today? Well, today I didn't do it!

Everyone needs recognition, affirmation, encouragement, help and support. When did you last stop thinking of yourself and give some out to those around you?

Reflection number 64

SEEING IT FROM A MAN'S PERSPECTIVE

When asked 'Who wears the trousers in your house?' Denis Thatcher (*the late husband of former Prime Minister Margaret*) was quoted as boldly replying, 'I do, and I also wash and iron them.'

There's a lovely story in Genesis where the woman was taken from the rib of the man while he slept. She wasn't taken from his head that she would be above him or superior to him in any way. She wasn't taken from his foot that she would be below him, or that she would be walked upon. The woman was taken from the man's rib just beneath his shoulder, from the centre of his body near to his heart, that she would be equal to him in every way and that he could always put his arm around her and comfort her.

My friends tell me that I always take the side of the woman in an argument—who knows, maybe I do? Perhaps it might have something to do with listening to so many tragic and appalling accounts from women over the years.

Hope you enjoy the following reflection—the title's at the top of the page. A friend of mine who's obviously married slipped it to me. It's funny, but like many stories that are funny, it contains a certain amount of truth.

It's really tough being a man! If you put a woman on a pedestal and try to protect her from the rat race, you're a male chauvinist. If you stay home and do the housework, you're a pansy.

If you work too hard, there is never any time for her. If you don't work enough, you're a good-for-nothing bum.

If she has a boring repetitive job with low pay, it's exploitation. If you have a boring repetitive job with low pay, you should get off your ass and find something better. If you get a promotion ahead of her, it's favouritism. If she gets a promotion ahead of you, it's equal opportunity.

If you mention how nice she looks, it's sexual harassment. If you keep quiet, it's male indifference. If you cry, you're a wimp. If you don't cry, you're totally insensitive and not in touch with your feelings like women are.

If you make a decision without consulting her, you're a typical male chauvinist. If she makes a decision without consulting you, she's a liberated woman. If you ask her to do something she doesn't enjoy, that's domination. If she asks you, it's simply a favour.

If you appreciate the female form, you're a pervert. If you don't, you're gay. If you like a woman to look beautiful and keep in shape, you're sexist. If you don't, you're unromantic. If you try to keep yourself in shape, you're vain. If you don't, you're a slob.

If you buy her flowers, you're after something. If you don't, you're not thoughtful. If she has a headache, she's tired. If you have a headache, you don't love her anymore.

If you're proud of your achievements, you're full of yourself, and if you're not, you simply have no ambition.

NO WONDER MEN DIE BEFORE WOMEN . . . . THE TRUTH IS— THEY WANT TO!

Reflection number 65

FREDDIE THE FROG

Two frogs accidentally fell into a bucket of cream. They swam around in circles for what seemed like ages, but sadly every effort they made to escape or to attract attention from passers by was all in vain.

Thinking that there was no hope, one of the frogs gave up, fell to the bottom of the bucket and drowned. The other frog, whose name was Freddie, was a different character completely. He was convinced that there had got to be a way out, and come hell or high water, he was determined to find it. He began splashing about frantically in the cream, trying to make as much noise as possible, in the hope that someone might hear him and come to his aid.

However, after a while he began to think he was dreaming—he couldn't believe his luck as he looked around and found himself sitting on top of a large lump of butter. He rested himself for a time to regain his strength, and as a soon as he felt well enough, he smiled and simply leaped out of the bucket.

It's a terrible thing for any of us to ever think or feel that there is no hope, after all there is always hope, no matter what situation we may or may not find ourselves in. Victory is always ours, but so often we are inclined to give up, just before the miracle takes place!

Reflection number 66

TIME FOR PRAYER?

Being human, we search for happiness and stability in our lives in different ways—unfortunately, it's often the case that we look in the wrong places. Some people turn to drink in the hope that it'll make them feel good and perhaps block out any problems that they may be experiencing. Others turn to prayer, because experience has taught them that at the end of the day it's the only thing that gets them through.

History has shown us that our ancestors have lived through many different ages. We had Stone Age, Iron Age and Bronze Age, to name just a few. It would seem today that we are living in the middle of 'Happy Age'. Everyone around us today wants to be happy, and is going to such huge lengths to ensure this 'look good and feel good factor'. Vast amounts of money are spent every day in an effort to look wonderful, hoping that if you look wonderful, you'll automatically feel wonderful too—sadly it doesn't always work out that way!

In Luke's gospel, chapter 11, a disciple asked Jesus to teach them how to pray. You could say that prayer is an 'out of fashion' thing today. It's not cool to say that we pray, or that we have faith, or that we go to church—much easier surely to plead agnosticism, or to stick the boot into all forms of organised religion. Admitting to having faith today is nearly something that people whisper, and afterwards amend their words by saying:—"Oh, I go to Church, but I'm not what you call holy or gospel greedy."

One thing is certain about prayer, the less you do, the harder it becomes. And maybe one of the reasons why many people find it so difficult to pray now, is not because it's out of tune with the times we live in, but simply because we've lost the skill of how to pray. If by chance you want the skill back again, you'll need two definite things—a time and a place.

Whilst everything we ask for in prayer is never going to come our way, prayer can give us something that's almost impossible to get anywhere else—inner peace. Why not give it a go?—All the best doctors recommend it—it's time out, it's therapeutic, and it doesn't cost a single penny. Hope you enjoy the reflection.

In my prayers I asked God for strength that I might achieve;
I was made weak that I might learn humbly to obey.
I asked for help that I might do great things;
I was given infirmity that I might do better things.
I asked for riches that I might be happy;
I was given poverty that I might be wise.
I asked for all things that I might enjoy life;
I was given life that I might enjoy all things.
I was given nothing that I asked for;
But everything that I hoped for.
Despite myself, my prayers were answered;
I am among all people most richly blessed!

Reflection number 67

LOVE CHANGES EVERYTHING

'*Darkness cannot drive out darkness; only light can do that. Hate cannot drive out hate; only love can do that. Hate multiplies hate, violence multiplies violence, and toughness multiplies toughness into a descending spiral of destruction. The chain reaction of evil must be broken, or we shall be plunged into the dark abyss of annihilation.*'—Dr. Martin Luther King Jnr.

During the Second World War Irmgard Wood lived in Germany. She tells the story that one morning her mother and sisters were out walking when they saw an American plane receive a direct hit and fall in flames from the sky. Irmgard's mother instinctively whispered a prayer for the pilot, even though in her country he was considered to be one of the enemy.

Years later Irmgard and her family emigrated to America, where her mother got a job working as a nurse in a local hospital. One day in the course of conversation a patient asked her what part of Germany she was from. When she said Stuttgart, he explained how he had a miraculous escape over Stuttgart during the war, when his plane suffered a direct hit and fell from the sky in flames.

'I got out in time. I just don't know how I did it, because I can never remember the details. To this day I am convinced that there was someone praying for me.'

More miracles are worked by prayer than the world ever dreams of. When you think about it, it's easy to pray for those who are good to us, just like it's easy to be kind to those who are generous towards us. However, it's a different story trying to be kind to someone who has hurt us, and it's difficult to pray for someone who has made life difficult for us in the past.

The gospel continually calls us to forgive those who have hurt us; and to love our neighbour—how many of us honestly do that? Hope this powerful gospel passage helps illustrate the point.

You have heard how it was said: You must love your neighbour and hate your enemy. But I say this to you: Love your enemies and pray for those who persecute you; in this way you will be children of your father in heaven, for he causes his sun to rise on bad people as well as good, and his rain to fall on dishonest people alike. For if you love those who love you, what right have you to claim any credit? Even the tax collectors do as much, do they not? And if you save your greetings for your brothers and sisters, are you doing anything exceptional? Even the tax collectors do as much, do they not? You must therefore be perfect just as your heavenly Father is perfect. (Matthew 5:43-48)

Reflection number 68

FAKES AND PHONIES

A young solicitor rented a magnificent office. To make an impression on any new clients that might come his way he bought a deluxe telephone. It sat impressively on his majestic marble desk waiting to be installed.

A client was announced—his first. The young solicitor deliberately made the poor man sit outside in the waiting area for half an hour, and in an effort to look busy and important he began to hold a fake telephone conversation as his client entered the room.

"Director general. My dear sir, we're both only wasting our time. Yes, if you absolutely insist—I'm sorry, not for less than ten thousand pounds. All right then, that's settled. Goodbye."

As he put the receiver down the solicitor noticed that his client looked baffled and confused. So, staring straight at him like the big bully that he was, he shouted abruptly:—"What can I do for you my good man?"

The man blushed, smiled and then replied:—"I know you're going to find this very embarrassing, but I've been sent to connect your phone."

Life is full of coco-pops! We meet them everywhere—they're the people who constantly try to impress, the people who use huge words; pronounce them incorrectly and put them in the wrong context. Sadly, they're also the people who don't realise that they treat their neighbours to a ringside comedy show every time they start boasting.

I remember once attending a posh party in a former parish where the hostess for the evening invited me to taste some of her homegrown strawberries that had been urinated that afternoon in Cointreau. Although I strongly suspect that the same strawberries were marinated in Cointreau, I nonetheless thought it prudent to pass up on the offer.

Isn't it such a pity that so many people do not feel secure enough to be themselves? The bible tells us that we are made in the image in the likeness of God—do we not believe that? Do we not believe that we are beautiful just the way we are? If we did, why then do so many of us feel the need to put on a fake performance when we meet someone on the street? Why do we constantly try to impress?

There's a lovely story told about an old missionary priest in Africa who needed an assistant. The religious order that he belonged to sent him a young scholar with a Ph. D. in Theology. When he arrived the young man had to speak to the locals through the old missioner, as he didn't really know the native language that well. In his first introduction to these simple, beautiful people, he delved deep into his learning and said, "Truth is absolute and relative. The gospel is absolute truth, but its application is relative to our immediate needs." He then paused for a moment for the old missioner to translate. The missioner frowned, rubbed his forehead, laughed heartily and said, "He says he's awful glad to be here."

The gospel and life are simple and beautiful—let's try not to complicate them and make fools out of ourselves!

Reflection number 69

POOR MARY

I'm reminded when Christmas is just around the corner by the post that arrives through my door. If it's not catalogues of flashy Christmas cards, its hotels and nightclubs begging me to book immediately for their Christmas Fayre. Aren't they so thoughtful, God love them, they're all worried that I might leave it too late, and find myself left out in the cold with nowhere to eat turkey, bop the night away and bump into inebriated and insufficiently dressed party goers.

Apart from all the silly malarkey that surrounds the festive season, I have to admit that I love Christmas. It really is a time of personal renewal, and of course goodwill and peace to all people—if we want it to be, that is? And just because other people race around the shops and stores before Christmas like headless chickens, it doesn't mean that you have to as well. To quote an old teacher from school, 'Would you put your hand in the fire just because someone else did?'

Why not make a promise to yourself that this year Christmas will be different, really different, and on top of that, promise yourself that you'll enjoy it more than ever before!

I had a dream Joseph. I don't understand it, not really, but I think it was about a birthday celebration for our son. The people had been preparing for it for about seven weeks. They had decorated their home and bought new clothes. They went shopping many times and bought elaborate gifts. It was peculiar though, because the presents weren't for our son. They wrapped them in beautiful paper and tied them with lovely bows and put them under a tree. Yes, a tree Joseph, right in the middle of their home. There was a figure on the top of the tree—it looked just like an angel in heaven might look, and yet their behaviour towards their neighbour was anything but angelic or heavenly. Everyone at the party was laughing and celebrating. They were so excited about the gifts. They gave gifts to each other Joseph, not to our son. Somehow I don't think they even knew him—they didn't mention his name once! Doesn't it seem odd for people to go to all that trouble to celebrate someone's birthday if they don't know him? I had the strangest feeling that if our Son had gone to this celebration He would have been intruding. Everything was so beautiful Joseph, but still it made me want to cry. How sad for Jesus not to be wanted at his own birthday party. I'm glad it was only a dream. How terrible Joseph if it had been real!

Reflection number 70

BECOMING A SAINT

November is a specific month in the Church when we remember our dead. We remember saints that the Church has proclaimed aloud, and we pray in a very special way for all those from our family and our neighbourhood who now rest with God. Their faces may not be on any stained glass windows in our churches, and their names may not be inscribed on any huge monuments around our city, but we know for sure that they are saints, because they touched our lives by doing the ordinary things of life in an extraordinary way—they showed us by example how to love God, and each day they lived out the commandment 'Love thy neighbour.'

Hope you enjoy the beatitudes—if we could try to live them, then perhaps in the future we too might be remembered as saints.

Blessed are those who strive to raise people up, not put them down.

Blessed are those whose work is done quietly and unassumingly, away from the glare of publicity.

Blessed are those who realise the value of each precious human being.

Blessed are those who make a great fuss of success and make little reference to failure.

Blessed are those who do not work simply for public acclaim or popularity.

Blessed are those who never lose sight of the really important things in life.

Blessed are those who show gratitude for the work that others do.

Blessed are those who do not trivialise what can look to some the most unimportant of jobs.

Blessed are those who realise that we are all more than just a number, that everyone has a great story to tell, and that we all deserve to be listened to.

Blessed are those who take raw materials, who mould them with love, who treat them with the utmost of respect, and who end up creating something of beauty and value, something that would never have been created if the materials had ended up in the hands of another.

Blessed are those who make such a difference in the lives of others, that it can never be measured in earthly terms—that is the greatest work that we can do.

Blessed are those who do God's work in the ordinary everyday situations of life—without them our world would be a poorer place.

Blessed are those who walk with God, because when you walk with God even through the worst of storms, you can always be sure that there is a rainbow waiting somewhere around the corner

Reflection number 71

THE BEREAVEMENT GROUP

One of the groups that I have been blessed to work with is the Bereavement Ministry in Newry Parish.

It's a small group of bereaved people who gather together every month and who offer each other support, consolation and kindness. The meetings consist of a wee prayer, some reflection, sharing and an informal chat with a 'cuppa'. Those who wish share their own personal experiences of grief and pain, and in doing so encourage others who wish to share in their turn. The group is interdenominational and totally confidential, and each person present can decide to either share or simply listen. To know that you are not alone in your grief, to know that others are journeying with you in your grief can sometimes be the first beginnings of healing.

Our Bereavement Ministers are just ordinary people—they are not perfect, they do not have the answers, and they are not completely healed of their own pain; but be assured that they will take the time to listen to you, to care for you, and they will be open and honest about their own journey through grief so that you might feel comfortable to be open and honest about yours.

Sooner or later grief comes to everyone. It is no respecter of persons. It comes to young and old, rich and poor alike. It can come suddenly and seem to swallow us up, or it can come slowly and bit by bit weigh us down like a millstone around our neck. Many parishes throughout the country have a Bereavement Support Group—be assured that you will be made very welcome there.

If you have a friend who is bereaved, let them know that a group such as this exists, and if you can, try to be a good listener and a good hugger—people in pain need genuine friends who will take the time to listen, and when necessary, put their arms around them!

Enjoy the reflection—*Hugging is healthy, it helps the body's immune system, cures depression, reduces stress and induces sleep. It is both invigorating and rejuvenating, and has no unpleasant side effects. Hugging is nothing less than a miracle drug—it lets people know that they're not alone and makes them feel loved.*

Hugging is totally natural, organic and sweet. It has no pesticides, no preservatives, no artificial ingredients and is 100% wholesome.

Hugging is practically perfect. There are no movable parts, no batteries to wear out and needs no periodic check-ups. It has low energy consumption, provides high-energy yield, is inflation proof, non-fattening, requires no monthly payments, no insurance premiums, is theft proof, non taxable, non polluting and is of course fully returnable!

Reflection number 72

KEEPING IT SIMPLE AND HONEST

One day a little girl was misbehaving at home. The little girl was the youngest in the family, and over the years her parents and her brothers and sisters had spoiled her. Because she was so used to getting her own way, she sulked or threw a tantrum when things didn't suit her. In an effort to teach her some manners, her mother told her to go and sit in the corner until her father arrived home. The little girl went over and stood in the corner, and in a symbol of rebellion, she refused point blankly to sit down on the chair.

The mother decided that she was not going to be dictated to by a five year old, and, after some sharp words, and might I add a little hassle, she finally managed to get her daughter to sit. A short while later the little girl's father arrived. He immediately noticed that his daughter was sitting in the corner with her arms folded and with her right foot tapping on the ground. When he asked her what she was doing, she replied, 'Well, on the outside I'm sitting down, but on the inside I'm still standing!'

'Spoiled little girl,' we might say, but aren't we all good at externals? How many of us can be seen to do the right thing all because we're under pressure to conform, and yet internally in our hearts there's something totally different going on. Surely we must admire the innocence of the little girl who told the truth? Let's be honest (like the child was), how many of us who profess to love our neighbours actually do?

Reflection number 73

ADVENT PREGNANCY STORIES

Chapter one of Luke's gospel is one of my favourites. We proclaim it every year during Advent—it's all about unexpected pregnancies!

Elizabeth, who is Mary's cousin, discovers after years of childless marriage that she is now pregnant. You can imagine that both Elizabeth and Zechariah must have been ecstatic—their prayers have been answered, and this baby is the most wanted baby in Palestine. I'm sure Elizabeth couldn't wait to tell the whole of the neighbourhood, especially those who made her life hell, and who made her feel humiliated because she had no children. Not every pregnancy brings that joy. Not every pregnancy has people rushing to shout it from the rooftops.

Let's move from the story of Elizabeth to the story of Mary. Mary is a young girl who is betrothed to Joseph; she is not married to him. And let's be honest about it, the same people who gossiped about Elizabeth's childlessness would have had an absolute field day if a young girl like Mary had a baby outside marriage. So, you can imagine what it must have been like for Mary to find an angel in her kitchen telling her that she was going to have a baby.

When I learned this story at school, I was told that Mary humbly submitted to the Lord's will and said "Be it done unto me according to thy word." In other words, she said "Yes, no problem, that's fine!"

If we look closely at that gospel story, the initial reaction of Mary is anything but meek and submissive. It is like the reaction of any woman or of any girl faced with a pregnancy that is not planned and not wanted. Luke tells us that Mary was bewildered trying to work out what was happening. It is only after she is totally reassured that God has willed the birth of this child, and that God will help her through the bad times ahead, that Mary finally says, "Yes, I accept this child."

Not a day in life goes by when some young girl or woman, married or single, finds herself facing a pregnancy which fills her with dread, fear, isolation and panic, instead of all the joyful feelings that Elizabeth experienced. Like Mary, many women are faced with the awesome question, am I willing to accept this child? And for all those women on their own; what happens next? Where are the angels? Where is God?

The answer is simple—we are the angels. We are told that we are the work of God's hands, so, we must do his work. We are the ones who are called to say, "Don't be afraid." We are the ones who are called to make the promises and say, "I'm here, and I'm going to help you!"

The gospel continually commands us to love—that means loving the born and the unborn. It commands us to love those who hurt us, who bring us pain, who refuse to take advice, and who get into trouble in spite of all our efforts and prayers.

It is easy to love those who never bring us anything but good news. We cannot possibly say that we are anti-abortion and at the same time gossip, tittle-tattle and condemn those who are pregnant. Such behaviour is total hypocrisy, and can often drive people to seek abortion. If we claim to be pro-life, we must be pro-life.

In the gospel Mary says, "Yes" to God. Let's hope that when we meet someone in trouble our first prayer will be, "Yes. Don't be afraid, for I'm going to walk with you, and I'm going to help you through this!"

November 1995

Reflection number 74

MEETING GOD FACE TO FACE

A little boy decided one day that he wanted to meet God. He had many questions going around in his head—What did God look like? Where did God live? Did God play games? What was God's favourite colour?

He guessed that it would probably be a long trek to God's house, so, he packed his rucksack with biscuits and several cans of coke before heading out on his journey.

As he walked down the road he came across an elderly lady sitting on a lonely park bench, watching the pigeons pottering around her feet. The boy sat next to her and opened his rucksack. He was about to take a drink from one of his cans of coke, when he noticed that the old lady looked sad—he offered her a few of his chocolate biscuits and she gratefully accepted. As she ate the biscuits she smiled at him. Her smile was so beautiful that he wanted to see it again, and so, he offered her a can of coke as well. Once again the old lady smiled at him, and the little boy was overjoyed.

The two friends sat together on the park bench all afternoon, eating and smiling, without saying a single word. As it grew dark the boy realised that it was time to go home. He got up to leave, but before he had travelled a few steps, he turned around, ran back to the old lady, and gave her a big hug. She gave him the biggest smile ever.

When the boy arrived home his mother was surprised by the look of joy on his face. She asked him, "What has made you so happy today, son?" He replied, "I had lunch with God." His mother began to laugh, but before she could say anything, he added, "And you know what? She's got the most beautiful smile in the whole world!"

Meanwhile, the old lady, also radiant with joy, returned to her home. Her son was stunned by the look of peace on her face. "Well Mother," he asked, "What has made you so happy today?" She replied, "I ate biscuits *and drank coke with God in the park today." And before her son could comment, she added, "And do you know something, he's much younger than I expected!"*

It's worth noting that when Christ came into the world not everyone recognized him. Do you think that still happens today?

Reflection number 75

THE TRUTH ABOUT CHRISTMAS

A young lad sat at the table doing his homework, while his father prepared the tea. "Daddy", called the boy, "where did I come from?" The father was unprepared for such a question. He stalled and coughed for a while, but eventually managed to answer, "A big stork brought you along."

A few moments later another question came. "So, where did you come from then, Daddy?" Once again the father was flustered, but managed to stammer out, "Well I was born around Christmas, so Santa Claus brought me, son."

The young lad continued writing in his homework book, but just as his father felt it was safe to relax a third question came along, "Well, if that's case, where did Grand-Dad come from then?" By this stage the father was almost beaten, but in desperation spluttered, "He was found under a cabbage at the bottom of the garden."

Later that night when the young lad had gone to bed, his father opened his homework book and read "As far as I can work out, there has not been one normal birth in this family for three generations."

Telling the truth, and facing the truth can at times be very difficult!

The truth about Christmas here in Ireland is that for many of us it is nothing more than a few days off work when we eat too much, drink excessively, spend foolishly and dance the nights away to Slade singing "Are you hanging up your stocking on the wall?"—Christ doesn't have any part in the equation.

It's a time in our country when Casualty wards are busier than ever before, when staff at 'Women's Aid' work overtime, and when 'St. Vincent de Paul' are run off their feet—sad, but fact!

If every January we wonder what the fuss was all about, if every Christmas all that we seem to get is a succession of rotten hangovers, sick stomachs and long lethargic experiences, then perhaps this year we might try to do something completely different and get to know 'this Jesus' whose birthday takes place on the 25th of December.

In truth, I can guarantee you'll find a friend like you've never had before—Why not give it a go? It'll sure beat some of your previous Christmas experiences!

Reflection number 76

OUR FRIEND JESUS

Two little lads sat in the garden on a hot afternoon, arguing with each other about prayer. "God never answers our prayers", one lad jeered. "Of course he does", the other disagreed. "Well then", said the first lad, "If you believe that, what happened last year? You prayed for a bicycle—remember? Did God answer your prayer back then?" The second lad thought for a moment, and then came back with, "Oh yes, he answered alright—it was just unfortunate that he said no!"

No is an answer, and if God were cruel and sadistic, he would say yes to our every prayer, and then he would laugh at us. But God is neither cruel nor sadistic and he will often refuse us what we ask for, because being a loving Father, he knows that in most cases, he has something much better to give.

I boast that my greatest achievement in the Priesthood was helping prepare a young boy by the name of Michael (God rest him) for First Communion. Michael was a pupil in Rathore School—his communication with me at all times was non-verbal. When in class, he just smiled at me, and at the end of each lesson he reached out for a big hug. After telling Michael stories about Jesus, colouring in pictures of Jesus, and watching videos about Jesus, I finally managed to get my hands on a mirror and I held it up in front of his angelic little face. "Now Michael", I said, "Where's Jesus?" Michael smiled and pointed at his reflection in the mirror. "Good boy", I said, "Well done, Michael!" Then I placed the mirror face down on the desk, folded my arms and said, "Now Michael, tell me, where's Jesus now?" Michael smiled again, and this time he pointed his finger at his heart. Bingo—the feeling for me at that moment was of profound reverence!

Children can teach us so much about Jesus in a very simple but powerful way. They see him as their best friend—when you think of it, what better relationship could any one of us have with Jesus?

A best friend will stand by us at all times—he or she mightn't always like what we do, but they will never stop loving us. Real friendship is everlasting—it's value can never be measured, and like good wine, as it matures, it's becomes even more beautiful, and so much more valuable.

Christ is indeed the perfect friend. I know of no better example of compassion, love, and understanding. He won't always agree with our lifestyles or the way in which we treat each other (*his gospel, if we take the time to read it, is certainly testament to that*), but being a real friend, he'll never walk away from us, or stop loving us, even if everyone else does.

Reflection number 77

RELAX WITH EACH OTHER AND WITH THE LORD

In Luke's gospel, chapter 10, there is a beautiful story told of two sisters—as different from each other as day and night. The first sister was called Martha, who it must be said, had a deep faith in God. Martha was a hard worker, and it would seem that she never stopped cooking, cleaning and praying—obviously one of those women who never had enough hours in the day, and who failed to realise that no-one is indispensable, and just about everyone can be done without.

Martha's sister Mary was the exact opposite—she welcomed Jesus into her home simply by sitting down and enjoying his company. Throughout His visit Mary listened to what Jesus had to say and relaxed in His presence—everything else for Mary was unimportant, especially housework.

The Gospels place great emphasis on doing good deeds, and yet, in this case, Jesus praises not the worker, but the one who sits down and listens. It wasn't that Jesus was scolding Martha—he was concerned for her. "Martha, Martha" he said "you worry and fret about so many things, and yet few are needed, indeed only one."

Jesus makes a point here for the benefit of all of us who are like Martha, people who are essentially generous and hardworking, but who are anxious and pre-occupied all the time about getting things done. It's not simply that Martha was busy, but that she was a complete slave to her duties.

There's a lovely story told about a father who was trying to read the newspaper one evening after he had come home from a rough day at work. As he attempted to turn the pages he found himself constantly interrupted by his children. One child came asking for money for an ice cream, while another child arrived into the room in tears—his leg was hurt, and he wanted his daddy to make it better. An older son came in with an algebra problem, and after much time and effort father and son arrived at the right answer.

Finally, the youngest child burst into the room, but by this stage her father was exhausted and wanted peace to be on his own. As he looked at his daughter standing there before him, he angrily asked her, "So, what do you want?" The little girl stood giggling for a while, and then, as she took his hand she whispered, "Daddy, I don't want anything. I just thought it would be nice if I could sit on you knee and we could relax together!"

This year, let's try and slow down a whole lot more—let's relax with each other and with the Lord. Believe it or not, life, God's greatest gift, is supposed to be enjoyed, not endured!

Reflection number 78

STICKY FINGERS

I remember at school (which doesn't seem all that long ago), the teacher talking to us about the need to be careful about where we set down our books, our schoolbags and our jackets—it appeared that there were certain boys in our school who had "sticky fingers". After working out what he meant by that expression, I have to admit that I giggled. I don't giggle today. Having been broken into twice, and having repeatedly listened to parishioners who have had their homes attacked, plundered and their personal possessions taken by thieves, I now find the very subject of pilfering repulsive. There's something horrible about having your home broken into—I suppose it has to be experienced to be really understood.

The amazing thing is that in this day and age thieving has actually become acceptable in some quarters—people even like to boast about their latest acquisitions. They laugh in company about the fact that they managed to get away with sneaking a glass or an ashtray from a local restaurant or hotel, and brag about how they got a real bargain from "a fella down the street" who sells televisions, stereos and DVD players for a quarter of the price that you'd get them in the shop.

It's strange that some people can hold their heads in an aloof manner, and for some reason consider themselves to be morally superior to the thieves who work the homes and the streets of our city each day, and yet they have no difficulty in personally seeking out those who sell clothes, furniture, computers and toys that are all 'knock-off'. If we participate in such scams, are we really any better than those who break into houses and shops, and who rob our poor old senior citizens? It's an old but wise saying, 'two wrongs will never make a right'!

It doesn't matter how anyone tries to justify it, the truth is simple—stealing will always be stealing, and will always be wrong. The Seventh Commandment states now as it did at the time of Moses, "Thou shalt not steal". And all the excuses in the world will never alter that simple fact!

Reflection number 79

I'LL BE HAPPY WHEN . . .

Isn't it amazing how many of us are not happy with our lives? There's nothing wrong—we haven't got sickness, a violent partner, serious financial problems, and we're not in trouble with the law. It's just that we're never really happy with what we've got—we always want more. And when more comes along, for some strange reason we want even more still!

No matter what the newspapers or television try to tell us about the latest product on the market, whenever we buy it, it just doesn't fill that gap—there's always something that's missing.

I suspect we've got it all wrong—God didn't give us all things to enjoy life; he gave us life to enjoy all things. We seem to have got the meaning of life back to front!

I hope this reflection is of some help—*We convince ourselves that life will be better after we get married, have a baby, then another. Then, we get frustrated that the kids aren't old enough, and we tell ourselves that we'll be more content when they are. After that, we're frustrated that we have teenagers to deal with. We will certainly be happy when they are out of that stage. We tell ourselves that our life will be complete when our spouse gets his or her act together, when we get a nicer car, when we are able to go on a foreign holiday or when we retire.*

The truth is there's no better time to be happy than right now. If not now, when? Your life will always be filled with challenges. It's best to admit this to yourself and decide to be happy anyway. Happiness is the way.

So, treasure every moment that you have, and treasure it more because you shared it with someone special, special enough to spend your time with . . . and remember that time waits for no one.

So, stop waiting . . . until your car or home is paid off. Until you get a new car or a new home. Until your kids leave the house. Until you go back to school. Until you finish school. Until you lose 10lbs. Until you gain 10lbs. Until you get married. Until you get a divorce. Until you have kids. Until you retire. Until Spring. Until Summer. Until Autumn. Until Winter. Until you die.

There is no better time than right now to be happy. Happiness is a journey, not a destination. So, work like you don't need money, love like you've never been hurt, and dance like no one's watching!

Reflection number 80

DONE WITH THE BEST OF INTENTIONS

Driving along a country road one evening I came across an old man bringing his cows home to milk. It was a lovely evening, and I was in no hurry whatsoever. As I watched I could see that the old man was balancing his bicycle with one hand and brandishing a stick in the other. On noticing that I was a priest he immediately set about making great efforts to help me overtake. And you know, I could have done that so easily, if he had just got out of the way—it would have been so simple just to edge past the cattle, if, of course, there had been no one there with them.

I sometimes think this must be the sort of experience that God suffers from most of all—those with the best intentions, must surely cause him the most bother!

Enjoy the reflection—apologies to all mothers with good intentions, who sometimes cause more harm than they do good!

1. My mother taught me RELIGION. "You better pray that stain will come out of the carpet, or you're for it!"
2. My mother taught me TO APPRECIATE A JOB WELL DONE. "If you're going to kill each other, do it outside. I've just finished cleaning."
3. My mother taught me LOGIC. "Because I said so, that's why."
4. My mother taught me FORESIGHT. "Make sure you wear clean underwear, just in case you're knocked down by a bus."
5. My mother taught me IRONY. Keep crying and I'll give you something to cry about."
6. My mother taught me about CONTORTIONISM. "Will you look at that dirt on the back of your neck!"

7. *My mother taught me about STAMINA. "You'll sit there until you have eaten all that spinach."*
8. *My mother taught me about WEATHER. "This room of yours looks as if a tornado went through it."*
9. *My mother taught me about HYPOCRISY. "If I told you once, I've told you a million times. Don't exaggerate!"*
10. *My mother taught me the CIRCLE OF LIFE. "I brought you into this world, and I can take you out."*
11. *My mother taught me about BEHAVIOUR MODIFICATION. "Stop acting like your father!"*
12. *My mother taught me ENVY. "There are millions of less fortunate children in this world who don't have wonderful parents like you do."*
13. *My mother taught me about ANTICIPATION. "Just wait until we get home."*
14. *My mother taught me about RECEIVING. "You are going to get it when you get home!"*
15. *My mother taught me MEDICAL SCIENCE. "If you don't stop crossing your eyes, they are going to freeze that way."*
16. *My mother taught me E.S.P. "Put your sweater on, don't you think I know when you are cold?"*
17. *My mother taught me HUMOUR. "When that lawn mower cuts off your toes, don't come running to me."*
18. *My mother taught me HOW TO BECOME AN ADULT. "If you don't eat your vegetables, you'll never grow up."*
19. *My mother taught me GENETICS. "You're just like your father."*
20. *My mother taught me about my ROOTS. "Shut that door behind you. Do you think you were born in a barn?"*
21. *My mother taught me WISDOM. When you get to be my age, you'll understand."*
22. *And my favourite: My mother taught me about JUSTICE. "One day you'll have kids of your own, and I hope they turn out just like you!"*

Reflection number 81

LOVE YOUR NEIGHBOUR

"Jesus said, 'You must love the Lord your God with all your heart, with all your soul and with all your mind. This is the greatest and the first commandment. The second resembles it: You must love your neighbour as yourself.'" Matthew 22:37-40

For me, failure to love one's neighbour is the greatest failure for a Christian.

There's a story told about a man who sold an old banger of a car to a poor unsuspecting stranger. The man boasted to his friends down at the pub that Friday night about how he had made a packet of money out of some poor eejit who had just bought himself a bundle of scrap—it was a great laugh for all those standing around. That Saturday night the same man went along to confession, and as he was coming out of Church, he met one of his mates from the pub who said to him, "I hope you told the priest how you cheated that poor man out of money with that old banger of a car you sold him." "I did no such thing," he replied, "I tell the priest my sins, but he has no right to know my business."

I am constantly surprised at the number of people I know who believe that they are Christians, and at the same time they don't speak to someone in their family, they have no problem in taking advantage of their neighbour, and they feel that they have some bizarre right to treat those around them as if they are nothing more than dirt.

The two commandments of love in our gospel are inter-related—true love of neighbour springs from the love of God; and there cannot possibly be love of God which does not express itself in love of one's neighbour.

There's an old story told about pre-integration days in America, where a tall black man was standing outside a Church that was attended by white people only. As it happened, the Church was very close to where he lived, and he was seriously considering attempting to go there on a Sunday morning rather than travel several miles to the all black Church where he was expected to attend. The story goes that as the man stood there looking around him, he met Jesus walking along. Jesus smiled at him and asked:—"What are you doing here?" The man paused for a moment and said:—"Well, to tell you the truth Jesus, I'm trying to figure out a way to get into this Church?" Jesus looked at him and began to laugh, saying:—"Oh, I know how you feel. I've been trying to work that one out for years as well!"

If we do not love our neighbour, can we possibly call ourselves Christians?

Reflection number 82

THE WOMAN'S CREED

It's an old and true saying that old habits die hard. Even though it's a few thousand years since Christ walked the Earth, and there are no Scribes and Pharisees about (well not literally speaking), life is still very much the same—women are still looked on by many as an inferior species. We rarely hear talk about adulterous men, it's usually always about adulterous women. And just as it's pointed out in John's Gospel (chapter 8), it's the women today who still earn the degrading titles; men are rarely, if ever, labelled. Men are still able to use women as they please, talk about them afterwards and walk away scot-free.

In the sight of God everyone is equal—men are not superior! In the book of Genesis it tells the story that the woman was taken from the rib of the man. She wasn't taken from his head that she would be above him, or from his foot that she would be below him to be trampled on. She was taken from his rib so that she would be equal, so that they could put their arms around each other and love each other.

Throughout the Gospels women have played a very silent, but a very significant and powerful role. Who gave birth to Jesus?—a woman. There may have been no women around the table at the Last Supper, but who do you think would have been in the kitchen preparing all the food?—women. And when our Lord was crucified, when one of the disciples denied knowing him, and all the others went into hiding for fear of their lives, who went to the tomb the very next day?—A few women of course! Who was the message of the birth of our Lord and the resurrection of Our Lord first revealed to—women!

Enjoy the woman's creed and let's try to think equality and live equality. *I believe in God who made woman and man in God's own image,* who created the world and gave both sexes the care of the earth. I believe in Jesus, child of God, chosen of God, born of the woman Mary, who listened to women and liked them, who stayed in their homes, who discussed the kingdom with them, who was followed and financed by women disciples.

I believe in Jesus who discussed theology with a woman at a well, and first confided in her his Messiahship, who motivated her to go and tell her great news to the city.

I believe in Jesus who received anointing from a woman in Simon's house and who rebuked the men guests who scorned her. I believe in Jesus who said this woman will be remembered for what she did, Minister of Jesus. I believe in Jesus who healed a woman on the Sabbath and made her straight because she was a human being.

I believe in Jesus who spoke of God as a woman seeking the lost coin, as a woman who swept seeking the lost. I believe in Jesus who thought of pregnancy and birth with reverence, not as a punishment—but as a wrenching event, a metaphor for transformation, born again, anguish into joy.

I believe in Jesus who spoke of himself as a mother hen who gathers her chicks under her wings. I believe in Jesus who appeared first to Mary Magdalene, who sent her with the bursting message "GO AND TELL" . . . I believe in the wholeness of the saviour in whom there is neither Jew nor Greek, slave nor free, male nor female, for we are all one in salvation. I believe in the Holy Spirit as it moves over the waters of creation and over the earth.

I believe in the Holy Spirit who like a hen created us and gave us birth and covers us with her wings!

Reflection number 83

THE WAY MEN SEE IT

I am frequently told that I am overly sympathetic towards women and much too critical of the men. Enjoy what some of our married guys have to say in the following reflection. As you might imagine, it's called "Rules from the Men."

1. Learn to work the toilet seat. You're a big girl. If it's up, put it down. We need it up, you need it down. You don't hear us complaining about you leaving it down. 2. Birthdays, Valentines, and Anniversaries are not a contest to see who can find the perfect present, yet again! 3. Sometimes we are not thinking about you—live with it please! 4. Shopping is 'NOT' a sport. And no, we are never going to think of it that way. 5. Crying is blackmail. 6. Ask for what you want. Let us be clear on this one: Subtle hints do not work! Strong hints do not work! Obvious hints do not work! Just say what you want! 7. We don't remember dates. Mark birthdays and anniversaries on a calendar—remind us frequently beforehand. 8. Most guys own three pairs of shoes. What makes you think we'd be any good at choosing which pair, out of thirty, would look good with your dress? 9. 'YES' and 'NO' are perfectly acceptable answers to almost every question. 10. Come to us with a problem only if you want help solving it. That's what we do. Sympathy is what your girlfriends are for. 11. A headache that last for 17 months is a problem—see a doctor! 12. Anything we said 6 months ago is inadmissible in an argument. 13. If you think you're fat, then you probably are. 14. Let us ogle. We are going to look anyway; it's genetic. 15. You can either ask us to do something, or tell us how you want it done—not both. If you already know best how to do it, just do it yourself. 16. Our relationship is never going to be like it was the first two months when we were going out—get over it and quit whining to your girlfriends. 17. All men see in only 16 colours. Peach, for example, is a fruit, not a colour. Pumpkin is also a fruit. We have no idea what mauve is. **18**. *We are not mind readers and we never will be. Our lack of mind-reading ability is not proof of how little we care about you.* **19**. *If we ask what is wrong and you say "nothing," then we will act like nothing's wrong.* **20**. *If you ask a question you don't want an answer to, expect an answer you don't want to hear.* **21**. *When we have to go somewhere, absolutely anything you wear is fine—really.* **22**. *Finally, remember that beer is as exciting for us, as handbags are for you!*

Reflection number 84

PROMISE YOURSELF

Not long after I was ordained, Father Dick O'Connell (R.I.P.) gave me some words of advice. He said, "Be nice to children, they have just come from God into our world, and be exceptionally nice to our senior citizens, they may soon be on their way from this world back to God.

Attending the sick and the housebound of our parish on the first Friday of the month is an incredible privilege—these beautiful people never cease to move me. I bring them the Blessed Sacrament, and they bring me to a much greater awareness of God's presence all around me. Every first Friday of the month for me is just like mingling with Angels. Paddy, who's one of my monthly calls, slipped me this reflection a fortnight ago. I hope it inspires you as much as it inspires me.

Promise yourself: To begin each day with a prayer of thankfulness upon your lips and a feeling of gratitude in your heart.

To look for the silver lining in each dark cloud and to acknowledge the many blessings in your life, no matter how small.

To nourish a positive attitude in your life and to see your difficulties as challenges and opportunities for personal growth.

To remove any bitterness from your heart towards another person and bless them upon their way.

To forgive, forgive and forgive.

To love those who have difficulty in loving.

To love and accept those parts of yourself which you have failed to do before.

To make constructive changes in yourself—now!

To tackle the job you have put off doing for weeks.

To be a better listener and not to judge.

To draw out the best in all your friends and to see beyond the confines of their personality.

To hug a friend and tell them how much you appreciate their friendship, either in the spoken word or in a letter.

To give your home and yourself a good spring clean and clear out all the clutter.

To buy or pick some flowers to give to a friend or to brighten up your home.

To give more of yourself to another than you have ever done before.

To turn off the T.V. more often, invite some friends round and communicate more.

To make a list of your good points.

To achieve something you find difficult.

To do something that makes you feel good about yourself.

To retire to your bed with a prayer of thankfulness upon your lips and a feeling of gratitude in your heart for the gift of life.

Reflection number 85

PENTECOST

A little girl went to stay with her grandmother in a small country town in America just outside New Orleans. One warm Sunday morning they both attended a very emotional religious service, where people expressed their feelings by jumping up and down and shouting; "Praise the Lord! Worship the Lord!" The little girl was puzzled as to what was going on around her, and so she asked her grandmother if all the jumping up and down and shouting praises to God meant that the Holy Spirit was present among them. Her grandmother, who was a wise old woman, squeezed the little girl's hand tightly and whispered into her ear, "Honey, it don't matter how high they jump up, it's what they do when they come down that will tell you if it's the real thing or not! They may be able to talk the talk, but can they walk the walk?"

The way in which we live our everyday lives will prove to those around us if we are Christians, hypocrites or pagans. It's very easy to talk about Christianity—let's face it, Irish people were always noted for being good talkers—the living out of our Christian beliefs is a different story completely.

The gifts of the Holy Spirit don't simply fly in on Pentecost Sunday and fly out again for another year—they are supposed to be present in our everyday lives, every single day.

In scripture we learn that when the Spirit came down upon the apostles they all began to speak in foreign languages. We don't need to speak different languages to prove we are Christians; we simply need to relate in a language of love to all the people around us—that's what really matters in God's eyes.

Perhaps today we might ask ourselves one basic question:—"If we were formally charged with being a Christian, would there really be enough evidence from our neighbours to convict us?"

Reflection number 86

CAN I DO ANYTHING RIGHT?

On a warm summer's morning, a farmer and his son headed into the nearby town with their donkey in tow. As they walked along the road they met a neighbour who stopped with them for a chat. "Where are you going?" he asked. "To the market," the farmer replied. "We have no use for this old donkey, and so we're going see if we can sell him for a few pounds that we might put to good use around the house." "The market's quite a distance away," said the neighbour. "Wouldn't you be better to get up on the donkey's back, and make the journey a bit easier for yourself?" The farmer thought that this was a great idea—his son walked alongside.

A few yards down the road they met another neighbour who immediately started to scold the farmer. "You big fat lazy lump," she shouted. "It's easy to see who does all the work on your farm. Imagine, the age of you up on top of that donkey, and your poor son having to walk—typical farmers, always exploiting and taking advantage of the younger generation!" The old farmer immediately slid off the donkey and told his son to take his place for the remainder of the journey.

No sooner had they turned the corner than they met a husband and wife who were out for their morning constitutional. Straight away, both began to laugh and said, "Well, we've seen it all." "It's the old dog for the hard road and the puppy for the path! There's no respect for age nowadays—would you look at that big fat ornament sitting up on top of the little old donkey, and his poor father having to walk!"

The farmer and his son looked at one another in amazement. "What shall we do?" the farmer said, "It would appear that we can't do right for doing wrong." "I've an idea," said the son. "Why don't we both sit on the donkey's back—that way no one can say we're doing anything wrong."

Unfortunately for them, a few yards later they came face to face with a very angry man who threatened to report them to the N.S.P.C.A. if they didn't immediately dismount. "I've never seen anything so cruel in all my life," he said, "have you no respect for that poor animal? What are you trying to do?" he asked, "Kill the poor thing?"

The farmer and his son stood bewildered on the country road. The market was due to start in a short while and they still had quite a distance to go. They were afraid of bumping into any more angry neighbours, so, they decided the best solution of all, was for both of them to lift the donkey up on to their backs, and carry it for the rest of the journey—that way, surely no one could complain anymore!

Sometimes, it would be best for everyone concerned, if we could all mind our own business!

Reflection number 87

THE STELLAS

I know this is hard to believe, but, in 1994 a New Mexico jury awarded $2.9 million in damages to 81-year-old Stella Liebeck who suffered third degree burns after spilling a cup of McDonald's coffee on herself. The case inspired an annual award—the "Stella" award for the most frivolous lawsuit in the U.S.

Let me tell you about a few of the candidates for "Stella". A jury awarded Kathleen Robertson of Austin, Texas, $780,000 after she broke her ankle tripping over a toddler who was running inside a furniture store. The owners of the store were understandably surprised at the verdict, considering the misbehaving little toddler was Ms. Robertson's son.

Jerry Williams of Little Rock, Arkansas, was awarded $14,500 and medical expenses after being bitten on the buttocks by his next-door neighbour's dog. The dog happened to be on a chain in its owner's fenced yard. The award was much less than Jerry had actually requested, as the jury felt the dog might have been just a little provoked at the time because Mr. Williams was shooting it repeatedly with a pellet gun.

A Philadelphia restaurant was ordered to pay Amber Carson of Lancaster, Pennsylvania, $113,500 after she slipped on a soft drink and broke her coccyx (tailbone). The beverage was on the floor because Ms. Carson had thrown it at her boyfriend 30 seconds earlier during an argument.

However, the best of all has got to be Mr. Merv Grazinski of Oklahoma City, Oklahoma. Mr. Grazinski purchased a brand new 32-foot Winnebago motor home. On his first trip home, having driven onto the freeway, he set the cruise control at 70 mph and calmly left the driver's seat to go into the back and make himself a cup of coffee. Not surprisingly, the vehicle left the freeway, crashed and overturned. Mr. Grazinski sued Winnebago for not advising him in the owner's manual that he couldn't actually do this.

The jury awarded him $1,750,000, plus a new 'Winnie'. After the lawsuit the company changed their manuals, just in case there were any consumers out there who didn't fully understand the Winnebago recreation vehicles actually worked.

Without doubt a huge compensation culture exists today in our world. In two motor accidents that I have been involved in (and let's be honest about it, they were my fault), both parties cleaned out my insurance—even though they swore to me at the time that they would never have anything to do with such skulduggery. I often wonder after an accident who people actually visit first—is it the doctor or the solicitor? If we are genuinely hurt—fine! But if we're not, if we put on an Oscar performance, if we embellish the injuries (i.e. tell lies), is that not stealing?

The Seventh Commandment states now, as it did when Moses came down from Mount Sinai, "Thou shalt not steal," and nothing in the world can ever alter that very simple, but profound truth!

Makes you think—no?

Reflection number 88

THE HONESTY OF YOUNG PEOPLE

On her way into Church last Sunday, a young person handed me the following reflection—she whispered to me that it summed up much of her feelings. It's called "Don't" and its great advice for parents.

Don't spoil me. I know quite well that I ought not to have what I ask for—I'm only testing you.

Don't be afraid to be firm with me. I prefer it—it makes me feel more secure.

Don't make me feel smaller than I am—it only makes me behave stupidly "big".

Don't correct me in front of people—I'll take much more notice if you talk quietly with me in private.

Don't make me feel my mistakes are sins—it upsets my sense of values.

Don't protect me from consequences—I have to grow up and I need to learn the painful way sometimes.

Don't be too upset when I say "I hate you"—it isn't you I hate, but your ability to sometimes drive me around the bend.

Don't nag—if you do, I shall have to protect myself by appearing deaf.

Don't forget that I cannot always explain myself as well as I would like to—that's why I'm not always very accurate.

Don't tax my honesty too much—I am easily frightened into telling lies.

Don't be inconsistent—that confuses me, and makes me lose faith in you.

Don't tell me my fears are silly—they are terribly real to me, and you can do much to reassure me if you just try to understand.

Don't put me off if I ask questions—if you do, you will find that I stop asking and seek my information elsewhere.

Don't ever think it is beneath your dignity to apologise to me—an honest apology makes me feel surprisingly warm to you.

Don't ever suggest that you are perfect or infallible—it gives me too great a shock when I discover that you are neither.

Don't forget how quickly I am growing up—it must be very difficult to keep pace with me, but please try.

Don't forget I love experimenting, I couldn't get on without it—so please put up with it.

And finally, don't forget that I cannot grow without lots of understanding love.

Reflection number 89

KEEPING IT SIMPLE

An old priest stood on the side of the road, gazing up at the spire of a new Parish Church that had just been opened. A little girl of about six or seven came up and stood beside him. Looking up into his face she asked, "Do you like our Church Father?"

"I do indeed," said the old priest, "it's very beautiful."

"Good," she said, "I'm so pleased, because you know, I actually helped to build it!"

"Really?" asked the old priest, "but you're only a wee girl—how could you help to build a Church?"

"Well," came the reply, "my daddy is a bricklayer, and he worked here at this Church ever since the building began, and every single day, me and my mammy brought him along his lunch!"

There is a great danger that we will all dream of doing something huge for God. However, God can often be best served in the most simple but real ways. It's very easy—all we have to do is open our eyes and see those in our family and in our community who are in need. Enjoy the reflection.

When old Mrs Hennessey opened the door,
Susan saw parcels and cards on the floor.
"It's my birthday", the old lady said with a smile,
"I'm here all alone. Can you stay for a while?"
Later while talking she grew very sad,
"This is the eightieth birthday I've had.
Each year I get parcels piled up in the hall,
but rather than parcels I'd love them to call.

I know you've worked hard at your School all day,
I'm sure you'd prefer to go out and to play.
I've beautiful cards on a line on the shelf,
but your present was best, because you gave me yourself!"

Reflection number 90

TAKE CONTROL OF THE SITUATION

It was a beautiful summer's day, and a young father pushed his screaming child around the park in his pram. While wheeling him up and down the various paths the father could be heard saying to himself:—"Easy now Jimmy, keep calm Jimmy, everything's all right Jimmy, just relax now Jimmy, you're doing just fine there Jimmy!" The child in the pram eventually settled down and went off to sleep.

A woman who was sitting on a bench nearby eating some sandwiches smiled up at the man and said:—"You certainly know how to deal with an upset child—gently and quietly always does the trick." The woman then leaned over the pram, smiled in at the child and whispered:—"Now, now, what was all that screaming for Jimmy?" The young father looked strangely at the woman for a few seconds and then blurted out:—"Oh no, no, I'm sorry. You've got it all wrong. The baby's called Peter, I'm the one who's called Jimmy!"

It's an old and true saying that the best way to take control of any situation is to take control over what's happening inside ourselves first. If we want to change a situation that we are unhappy with, we might begin by asking, "What can I do to change here?"

I've always believed that there really is no excuse for bad manners, bad tempers or bad behaviour from anyone, and those who are willing to accept rudeness, vulgarity, crankiness and offensive behaviour as part of another person's make up, are merely giving them permission to continue.

Some time ago I attended a wedding reception and sat in absolute horror as the best man (who was the groom's best friend) told blue joke after blue joke and almost likened the bride to a prostitute. Everyone sat there in silent submission letting him rave on and on, in what must have been the most singularly embarrassing experience for the bride, her family and the guests. However, what shocked me most was that no one from his family took the microphone away from him, no one told him that his behaviour was totally unacceptable, no one got up and walked out—in fact no one did anything—except laugh or pretend that it didn't happen.

Anyone of us could surely look at our lives at times and say, "Jesus deserves something better from me than this." If we don't like what's going on around us, we can do something that is very simple and yet very profound—remove ourselves from the situation! Very often silence is not golden—it is yellow, and if we stand by and do nothing while someone's character is assassinated or made a laugh of, we are allowing ourselves to take part in an action that is totally un-Christian.

Reflection number 91

THE GOOD OLD DAYS

Would I like to be young again? The answer is most definitely "No". Children today certainly enjoy a different lifestyle than I ever did, but it's not a better lifestyle!

A friend of mine sent me the following article. If you can identify with it—great! If not—you really are the loser!

According to today's regulators and bureaucrats, those of us who were kids in the 50's, 60's, and 70's shouldn't have survived. Why?—Well, our baby cots were covered with brightly coloured lead-based paint which we all promptly chewed and licked. We had no childproof locks on our medicine bottles, or kitchen cabinets, and it was fine then to play with pots and pans.

When we rode our Daisy-bell bicycles we wore no helmets, just plastic sandals bought from the market and fluorescent 'clackers' on the wheels. As children, we would ride in cars without seat belts or air bags—sitting in the passenger seat was a real treat. We drank water from the garden hose, and it tasted great. We ate dripping sandwiches, bread and butter pudding and drank fizzy lemonade with sugar; however, we were never overweight, because we were always outside playing.

We shared one drink between four friends, all from the one bottle, and no one actually died from this. We would spend hours building go-carts out of scraps and then fly at top speed down the hill, only to find out we forgot the brakes. After running into stinging nettles a few times, we learned to solve the problem. We would leave home in the morning and play all day, making sure we were back before it got dark. No one was able to reach us all day and no one minded.

We didn't have play-stations, video games, 99 channels on TV, videotape movies, surround sound, mobile phones, personal computers or

Internet chat rooms—we had friends! We played elastics and rounders, and sometimes that ball really hurt. We fell out of trees, got cut and broke bones and teeth. There were no lawsuits—they were accidents. We had fights, punched each other hard and got black and blue—we learned to get over it. We walked to all our friend's homes.

We rode bikes in packs of 7 and wore our coats just by the hood. The idea of a parent bailing us out if we broke a law was unheard of. Parents actually sided with the law—imagine that! Our generation has produced some of the best risk-takers and problem solvers and inventors, ever. We had freedom, failure, success and responsibility, and we learned how to deal with it all.

Is life really any better for young people today?

Reflection number 92

ARE YOU UP FOR THE JOB?

Enjoy the reflection—*The Lord said to me, "Go!" And I said, "Who, me?" And he smiled at me and said, "Yes, you!" And I said, "Oh but I couldn't, we have visitors coming, and the kids need me, and sure there's no-one to take my place here at home or at work!" The Lord smiled at me then and said, "Are you sure about that?"*

A second time the Lord said, "Go!" And I said, "But I don't want to." The Lord smiled at me again and said, "I didn't ask you if you wanted to!" So I said, "Listen Lord, I'm not the kind of person who gets involved like that. Besides, my family might not like it, and the neighbours will all think I'm a goody-goody!" The Lord smiled at me once more and said, "Listen, I know all about it!"

A third time the Lord said, "Go!" And I said, "Do I have to?" The Lord asked, "Do you love me?" And I said, "Look Lord, I'm really scared. I don't know how to do this type of work, and people all about me won't understand, and I just feel that I can't do it all on my own!" The Lord laughed and said, "And where do you think I'll be?"

A fourth time the Lord said to me, "Go!" So I smiled at him this time, and replied, "Here I am Lord, send me!"

God calls all of us to be messengers of his love. It's not a difficult job by any manner or means. You don't have to reek of incense or drip of candle-wax—human beings who fall very often, who are only too aware of their own imperfections usually make the best candidates, as thankfully they are not prone to judging others!

If you think that you're not up to the job, take a look at some of the characters from the Bible that God depended upon—Moses stuttered, Timothy had a problem with his stomach, Jacob was a liar, David had an affair, Abraham was too old, John was self-righteous and Naoimi was a poor widow. Paul was a murderer, Jonah ran away from God, Miriam was a gossip, Gideon doubted (so did Thomas), Jeremiah was depressed and suicidal, Elijah was burned out, Martha was a worrier and Amos' training was in fig tree pruning.

God needs all of us to pass on his message. Why not give it a go?—whoever you are!

Reflection number 93

BUMPER STICKER TALK

Chat Show Hosts seem to be almost famous nowadays for "Bumper Sticker" conversations—if they're not refereeing fights they're advising you to "take a swim in Lake You!" If you're one of those people who enjoy a daily dose of Kilroy, Rikki Lake or Jerry Springer then you'll probably have heard of some of the following. Enjoy:

Women's Bumper Stickers:—*1. So many men, so few can afford me. 2. God made us sisters—Prozac made us friends. 3. My mother is a travel agent for guilt trips. 4. Local Princess having had sufficient experience with many local Princes; now seeks frog. 5. Coffee, chocolate, men . . . some things are just better rich. 6. Don't treat me any differently than you would the Queen. 7. Warning: I have an attitude and I know how to use it. 8. Of course I don't look busy . . . I did it right the first time. 9. Do not start with me mate—You will not win. 10. Sorry if I looked interested—I'm not. 11. If you want breakfast in bed, sleep in the kitchen.*

Men's Bumper stickers:—*1. I love you not because of who you are, but because of who I am when I'm with you. 2. No man is worth your tears, and the one who is certainly won't make you cry. 3. Just because someone doesn't love you the way you want them to, doesn't mean they don't love you with all they have. 4. A true friend is someone who reaches for your hand and then touches your heart. 5. The worst way to miss someone is to be sitting right beside them, knowing that you can't have them. 6. Never frown, even when you're sad—you'll never know who's falling in love with your smile. 7. To the world you may be just one person, but to one person you may be the whole world. 8. Don't waste your time on a man/woman who isn't willing to waste their time on you. 9. Maybe God wants us to meet a few wrong people before meeting the right person, so that when real love finally happens; we'll know how to be truly grateful. 10. Don't cry because it's over, smile because it happened. 11. Don't try too hard—the best things in life come when you least expect them.*

However, the one that's best to pin up on your refrigerator, write on your text book and repeat silently every day has got to be: *"God grant me the serenity to accept the things I cannot change, courage to change the things I can, and wisdom to know the difference!"*

Reflection number 94

MAKING IT POSSIBLE FOR YOU TO ATTEND CHURCH

Not attending Church on a Sunday has become really fashionable for so many people—some now even boast about it. On television some celebrities make fun of the sacraments, and see no need for marriage or even God for that matter.

I remember some years ago visiting a home where an elderly man took great delight in telling me that he hadn't attended Church for many years. When I asked him would he foresee a time in the future that he might once again join us for worship, he growled at me, "never!" "Why so?" I asked. "Are we really that bad?" ""Well," he said, "If you ask me all those who attend your Church on Sunday are nothing more than a bunch of hypocrites, and I want nothing to do with any of them!" "Mmmm," I replied, "that might certainly be the case, but remember that we'll always have room for one more—that is, if you want to join us!"

Our Church, like all Churches, is a very human Church, and that's the way it's always going to be! We don't always get it right (that's for sure), but then again we don't always get it wrong. We work with people on a daily basis in the most bizarre and most unimaginable situations—many of them have chosen not to practice their faith, and we hope that in some small way we're helping them. If you're one of those people who has lapsed and would like to come back, be assured of a warm welcome waiting for you. If you're happy enough to stay away, be assured that we're still here to help you in some way, that is, if we can.

Enjoy the reflection—it's humorous but good: *To make it possible for everyone to attend our Church next Sunday, we're going to make it very special.*

A bed will be placed in the Sanctuary for those who say, "Sunday is my only day for sleep."

Eye drops will be available for those with tired eyes from watching television too late the night before.

Steel helmets will be on offer for all those who say, "The roof would cave in if I came to Church."

Blankets will be furnished for those who think that the Church is too cold, and fans will be on hand for those who say that it's much too hot.

Hearing aids are accessible for all those who say that the priest speaks too softly, and cotton wool for those who complain that the priest shouts.

Scorecards will be placed at the edge of each seat for listening hypocrites who are present.

Hot TV dinners will be available for collection immediately after Church for all those who can't go to Church and cook dinner as well.

A selection of trees and grasses will be in the porch for all those who like to see God in nature.

A putting green will be placed beside the Altar for all those who say, "Sunday is my only day for golf."

And finally, the Sanctuary will be decorated with Christmas poinsettias and Easter lilies for all those who have never seen Church without them.

Think you might like to join us?

Reflection number 95

STREET ANGELS AND HOUSE DEVILS

I met an old friend of mine one day for lunch. After a few glasses of wine we got around to talking about friends and family, who you relate really well with in your family and who drives you around the bend. My friend's father has been dead for years, something that didn't seem to bother him at all. He didn't know his father personally—his parents had been separated for as long as he could remember. He told me that some time ago he had called into a shop in the town where his father had been raised. As he was writing out a cheque to pay his bill the shop assistant read his name on the bottom of the cheque and said to him:—"My God, are you John???" He replied, "Yes, yes I am," thinking that he had met this girl on holidays a few years previously. "Gosh" she said, "You'll never believe it—we're cousins! Your father and my mother were brother and sister." "Good God," he said, "that's amazing." "Yes, isn't it?" she gasped. "You know, your father was a great man. Gosh, he was so much fun and incredibly kind—he would have done anything to help people."

By this stage my friend had had enough and said, "Well, that's amazing—he was kind, imagine that? Funny, he left us when I was a baby and we never ever heard tell of him again. He crucified my mother, but I'm really glad he was nice to someone else. I'm told by my brothers and sisters that he would be best described as a street angel and a house devil—always had to be the King of the castle, and whenever he wasn't treated like a King at home, my God did my mother suffer for it! But, I'm glad he was good to someone—he certainly wasn't good to us!"

It's a sad fact of life, but it's a very true one we have many street angels and house devils in our villages, towns and cities. I have no doubt that every parish has its fair share of wives, husbands and children, who if the truth be told, haven't got the living of a dog in their own home. And yet to everyone outside, they give the impression of being the perfect happy family. There are many in the community who are power freaks, who treat the people that they live with and work with like dirt. For some bizarre and weird reason they have to be the "King" of "Queen" of their castle all the time.

The kingdom that Jesus talked about so often in the Gospel was one of love—a love that is expressed in sharing, understanding, respect, equality and goodness. There could be no room in his kingdom for selfish people, for injustice or for anyone who made life difficult or painful for those around them. When Christ talked about being a King, he talked about a person who preferred to serve, rather than be served and he told us that the greatest commandment of all was to love. In fact, he could barely tolerate the Pharisees who lorded their authority over others and who made life difficult for people—it was Christ who coined the phrase that they were nothing but a bunch of hypocrites.

Does the cap fit?

Reflection number 96

OLD HABITS DIE HARD

Once upon a time a King was walking through the streets of his capital city when he came upon a beggar who asked him for money. The King refused the beggar's request, but instead invited him to his Palace. The beggar happily took the King up on his offer.

On the appointed day as he made his way through tight security the beggar felt both embarrassed and ashamed—as he looked around him he became acutely aware of the way that he looked, and what his shabby clothes represented.

The King, who was an exceptionally kind person, received the beggar man warmly, and taking pity on him he fed him, clothed him and bestowed him with many gifts—among them was a new set of warm, smart clothes. However, a few days later the very same man was back on the streets dressed in rags and begging once more.

Sadly, the beggar man gave away his new clothes because he knew that in order to wear them he would have to live a new life—this, he was just not prepared to do. Unfortunately, he was too steeped in habit, and change for him would involve much pain and uncertainty—it was easier for him to simply stay the way he was.

Habit plays a big part in all our lives. It is said that we live the second half of our lives according to the habits formed in our first half.

Let's be blatantly honest here, it's really difficult to say goodbye to a selfish lifestyle, and to break bad practices—even though we know them to be wrong. Isn't there an old proverb somewhere that says: "Old habits die hard"?

One of the main calls of our gospels is repentance. Repentance is more than just being sorry for what we've done; it's also about trying to make permanent changes in our lives that will help us not to repeat the same mistakes over again.

It might be good today to stop, and perhaps name some of the areas in our lives where we need to bring repentance. It may only seem like a small step to some of us, but let's remember that great journeys always begin with small steps, and they are steps in the right direction. On the other hand, we could choose to be like the beggar man in the story, and not be prepared to make any effort at all.

What will you do?

Reflection number 97

THE APOSTLES

Experts and Business Gurus today seem to be great advocates of psychological testing in order to gauge the effectiveness of personnel in an organisation. It is widely suggested that if Jesus had sent his twelve disciples for the above tests this might well have been the reply he would have received:

"Chief Executive Christ, thank you for submitting the resumes of the twelve men you have picked for managerial positions in your new organisation. All of them have completed our series of examinations. Naturally we have run all results through our computer, and after having arranged interviews for them with our psychologist, it is the opinion of our staff that most of your nominees are lacking in background, basic education and vocational aptitude for your enterprise. It is obvious that this group have no team concept whatsoever.

We would like to draw to your attention that Simon Peter is emotionally unstable and prone to fits of temper. Andrew, his brother, has no qualities for leadership. The other siblings, James and John, place personal interest above company loyalty, and Thomas shows a sceptical attitude that would most certainly undermine all group morale. We wish to point out that Matthew has been blacklisted by the 'Jerusalem Better Business Bureau' while James the son of Alphaeus and Thaddeus most definitely has radical leanings and register a high score on the manic depressive scale.

One of your candidates however shows real potential. He is a man of ability and resourcefulness. His social skills are indeed outstanding and we note that for someone so young he has many contacts in high places. Without hesitation we would recommend Judas Iscariot as your leader, controller and right hand man."

Thank God that our effectiveness as Gospel people has nothing to do with our skills or our individual talents—it is all about the spirit of God working in and through us. And when you put it like that, absolutely anyone can be a disciple.

Please, take up His challenge!

Reflection number 98

DON'T CONFUSE THE MESSENGER WITH THE MESSAGE

Encouraging people to attend Church at present is indeed a mammoth challenge. Sadly, today some will only grace us with their presence if they are moved by the messenger, rather than the message. Others, I find, can come up with ten million valid reasons why not to attend, and naturally none of their reasons involve them making any effort. Realistically, it's impossible to cater for everyone in our Church at the same time, or to even try for that matter, especially as our parishioners are much like our priests—they all differ in huge ways (and thank-God for that)!

The following is a summary of local comments made about a priest in a typical Irish parish:

If his sermon is longer than usual: "He sends us all to sleep!"
If it's short: "He hasn't bothered to make an effort!"
If he raises his voice: "He's shouting!"
If he speaks gently: "You can't hear a thing!"
If he's away from the parish: "He's always on the road!"
If he's at home: "He's a stick in the mud!"
If he's out visiting: "He's never at home!"
If he's in the presbytery: "He never visits his parishioners!"
If he talks about finances: "He's too fond of money!"
If he doesn't: "The parish is dead!"
If he takes his time with people: "He wears everyone out!"
If he is brief: "He never listens!"
If he starts Mass on time: "His watch must be fast!"

If he starts a minute late: "He holds everybody up!"
If he is young: "He lacks experience!"
If he is old: "He ought to retire!"
And if he dies? "Well, of course, no one could ever take his place!"

If you can afford some time off to stop and listen, you'll notice that there are many people around you who spend their lives blaming others for everything that's wrong with themselves. I suppose if we don't want to hear, or listen, or accept responsibility, then it's natural that we'll always find some sort of excuse—the blame game is a very popular game here in Ireland!

Whatever arguments or debates or discussions you want to get involved with about your Church or your priest/minister, do so—it's very healthy to put your point of view across, and of course to feel that you're respected and listened to. But whatever you do, please, make sure that you never ever confuse the messenger with the message!

Reflection number 99

DO I MAKE SENSE?

Do you ever wonder . . . Why the sun lightens our hair, but darkens our skin? . . . Why women can't put on mascara with their mouth closed? . . . Why you don't ever see the headline "Psychic Wins Lottery"? . . . Why "abbreviated" is such a long word? . . . Why doctors call what they do, "practice"? . . . Why you have to click on "Start" to stop Windows 98? . . . Why lemon juice is made with artificial flavour, while dishwashing liquid is made with real lemons? . . . Why the man who invests all your money is called a broker? . . . Why there isn't mouse-flavoured cat food? . . . Why Noah didn't swat those two mosquitoes? . . . Why they sterilise the needle for lethal injections? . . . Why they don't make the whole aeroplane out of the same material used to make the indestructible black box? . . . Why sheep don't shrink when it rains? . . . Why they are called apartments when they are all stuck together? . . . Why if con is the opposite of pro, then how come congress is the opposite of progress? . . . Why they call the Airport "the Terminal", if flying is so safe?

Do you ever wonder how there can be constant burglaries, robberies, vandalism, killings and abuses here in our city, when everyone has heard about Christ and his teaching about "Love of one's neighbour"? Like all the rest, it just doesn't make sense—does it?

Perhaps instead of trying to work out the above, we could take a look at our own lives (and especially the ways in which we treat our families and neighbours) and then ask ourselves:—Do we make sense? Are we a puzzle, because we claim to be Christians and we act like complete pagans? If we talk about love, but often live in hate, then it would seem that our lives are like the silly bumper stickers—total contradictions!

However, the good news is that it's never too late to change!

Reflection number 100

RELY ON OLD-FASHIONED EXPERIENCE

While O-Levels, A-Levels, Spirit Levels and Degrees are certainly not to be sniggered at, when it comes to wisdom there really is nothing that can quite match good old-fashioned experience. The world famous boxer Muhammad Ali was once quoted in an interview as saying, "The man who views the world at fifty in the same way as he did at twenty has certainly wasted thirty years of his life!"

Personal experience always comes at a cost, and often that cost is time, heartache, pain and the making of many mistakes. However, there are certain guarantees with all that pain that has to be got through—and they are, you'll never ever forget your mistakes, and you'll sure as hell try never to repeat them again. Could such wisdom possibly be learned from a book?—Personally, I think not! For that reason our senior citizens are undoubtedly our greatest assets—can you imagine the real life stories that they could tell?

Enjoy the reflection—Eleanor Roosevelt wrote it from her own personal experiences: *"Many people will walk in and out of your life, but only true friends will leave footprints on your heart.*

To handle yourself, use your head; to handle others, use your heart. Remember in all situations that anger is only one letter short of danger. If someone betrays you once, it's their fault; if that same person betrays you twice, then it's your fault.

Beautiful young people are accidents of nature, but beautiful old people are truly works of art. Always look around you and try and learn from the mistakes of others—you can't live long enough to make them all by yourself.

Note that great minds discuss ideas; average minds discuss events; and only small minds discuss people. The person who loses money loses much, the person who loses a friend loses much more, but the person who loses faith in God loses everything!"

Reflection number 101

NO ONE IS INDISPENSABLE

Funerals are what some people would call "big business." Take a look around you and you'll see luxurious limousines ferrying bereaved family members all the way to Church and back. Hand in hand with such opulence go shiny oak coffins draped with white weeping lilies, priceless marble headstones awaiting expensive gold lettering, and hotel function rooms ready to accommodate relatives and friends with the finest cuisine that Ireland can possibly offer. However, for all that funeral personnel are able to arrange, they still haven't worked out how to attach your house on to the end of the hearse, and bury it alongside your remains in the cemetery.

While we're expected to give of our best at all times, it's important to remind ourselves frequently that none of us are indispensable, and that everything we accumulate in this world has to be left behind when we die—property, wealth, prestigious titles, positions and all else that you can dream up or think of.

I often wonder is there some sort of insecurity in people who want to have their names engraved on a huge stone monument, or on the wall of a public building, so that they, and the service they once provided, might be long remembered and talked about for years and years to come. What sort of a need is there in people like that? Surely it's a much nicer option just to be remembered in the hearts of our family and our neighbours as someone who cared, who didn't judge, and who always had time for others.

Enjoy the reflection—it's for all of us who think that we can't be done without—remember, "he who works and does his best, goes down the road like all the rest!"

Some time when you're feeling important, sometime when your ego's in bloom, sometime when you take it for granted you're the most qualified man in the room, sometime when you feel that your going would leave an unfillable hole, just follow these simple instructions and see how they humble your soul.

Take a bucket and fill it with water, put your hands in it up to the wrists, pull them out—and the hole that remains, is the measure of how much you'll be missed. You may splash all you please when you enter, you may stir up the waters galore, but stop, and you'll find in a minute, that it looks just the same as before.

The moral of this story is simple—you must do the best that you can, be proud of yourself, but remember, "there is no indispensable man!"

Reflection number 102

FORGIVING AND MOVING ON

A woman died and made her way to the gates of Heaven. While waiting to meet up with "good old Saint Pete", she peeked in and saw a beautiful banquet table. Sitting all around were her parents and all the other people she had loved and who had died before her. They immediately recognised her and began calling greetings to her "Hello—how are you? We've been waiting for you! Great to see you!"

When Saint Peter arrived the woman smiled and said to him, "This is such a wonderful place! How do I get in?" "Well, you have to spell a word," Saint Peter told her, "and if you spell it correctly, the gates will automatically open for you!" "What's the word?" the woman asked. "Oh it's very simple" he said, "the word we're looking for here is Love." The woman correctly spelled "Love", and Saint Peter welcomed her into Heaven.

Some years later Saint Peter came to the same woman and asked her to keep watch at the Gates for him that day—it seemed that he had some other business to attend to. While the woman was standing guard she noticed in the distance her husband walking towards her. "My goodness, I'm surprised to see you," she said. "How have you been?" "Oh, I've been doing pretty well since you died," her husband laughed. "I married that pretty young nurse who took care of you while you were ill. Of course it goes without saying that I won the National Lottery and sold the little house you and I lived in. It seemed only right for me to buy a huge mansion—it really is a sight to behold! My new wife and I have travelled all around the world. We were on vacation in the Caribbean today when I took a crazy notion to go water skiing. Tragically I fell and hit my head on a huge rock, and lo and behold here I am. What a bummer! By the way, how do you get these gates to open?"

"Well, it's all very magical", the woman stammered. "You have to spell a word, and if you spell it correctly the gates will automatically open. But,

if you spell it incorrectly, then sadly I'm afraid it's down below, with no hope of return!" "Well, what's the word I have to spell then?" her husband asked. The woman thought for a moment and then quietly seethed, **"Czechoslovakia!"**

The moral of the story: Never make a woman angry . . . there'll be Hell to pay later!

I'm sure like myself you'll have noticed all the shops around the place getting ready for Christmas, trying to lure us in and spend our every last penny. Perhaps before we make out our lists of what to buy for this festive season, we might make a list of those in our family and in our community that we need to make peace with first!

Reflection number 103

IF JESUS CAME TO YOU THIS CHRISTMAS

Am I just getting old or is time flying? Can you believe it?—Christmas lights are well and truly lit, Santa Claus is firmly established in his grotto, and the official countdown to December 25th has once again begun.

Amid all the festive fun and parties that we somehow feel our lives would be incomplete without, let's make sure that we create some space in our lives for Jesus too. Tragically, many of us seem to have turned into modern day Bethlehem Innkeepers—we have no room in our homes or our lives for Jesus. Enjoy the reflection.

If Jesus came to you this Christmas:
Would you have to change your clothes before you let him in?
Or hide your magazines, and put the Bible where they had been?

Would you hide your worldly music and put some hymnbooks out?
Could you let Jesus walk right in, or would you have to rush about?

Well I wonder, if the Saviour spent a day or two with you,
Would you go on doing the things you always do?

Would you go right on saying the things you always say?
Would life for you continue as it does from day to day?
Would you take Jesus with you everywhere you go?
Or would you maybe change your plans just for that day or so?

Would you be glad to have Him meet your closest friends?
Or would you hope they all stayed away, just until His visit ends?

Would you be glad to have Him stay forever on and on?
Or would you sigh with great relief when He at last was gone?

It might be interesting to know, the things that you would do,
If Jesus came at Christmas to spend some time with you?

Reflection number 104

POOR PEOPLE

It looks as if the Christmas rush has begun—crispy bank notes and shiny visa cards are being pushed across shop counters all around our city and parents are out in force, armed with lists of expensive requests ranging from mobile phones that take your photograph, to designer trainers which begin at around £90.00 (Whatever happened to shopping in the market for a pair of gutties that only cost around £2.50?). While we continually spoil our children with the very best that money can buy (and with what we never would have received in a month of Sundays), we might ask ourselves one very important question: "Are we really doing our children any favours?" While we might be rearing them with much more than our parents reared us, are we rearing them any better?

Enjoy this story. One day the father of a very wealthy family took his eldest son on a trip into the country with the purpose of showing him how "poor people" lived, and also to illustrate to him just how lucky he and his family were to be blessed with so many riches. Together they spent a few days and nights on the farm of what was considered to be a very poor family indeed.

On their return home, the father asked his son, "Well, how was your trip?" "It was great Dad" he replied. "Were you amazed at just how poor some of the people were?" his father asked. "Oh yes, absolutely", said the son. "Well then, tell me?" asked the father, "What exactly did you learn from your adventure?"

The son thought for a moment and then answered, "Well, I saw that we have one dog and they had four. We have a pool that reaches to the middle of our garden while they swim in a river that has no end. We have imported lanterns in our garden while they have the stars at night. Our patio reaches to the front yard, yet they have the whole horizon. We have a small piece of land to live on and they have fields that go way beyond our sight. We have servants who serve us, but they serve each other. We buy all our food and they grow their own. We have walls around our property to protect us; they have family and friends to protect them". The boy's father was speechless. Then his son added, "Thanks, Dad for showing me just how poor we really are!"

Too many times we forget just how much we really have, and concentrate on what we don't have—what is one person's worthless object is another person's prize possession—it's all based on perspective. Makes you wonder what would happen if we all gave thanks for the riches and blessings we already have, instead of constantly wanting more!

Reflection number 105

COPPING ON

If you can start the day without caffeine,
If you can be cheerful, ignoring aches and pains,
If you can eat the same food everyday and be grateful for it,
If you can understand when loved ones are too busy to give you time,
If you can overlook when people take things out on you,
If you can take criticism and blame without resentment,
If you can face the world without lies and deceit,
If you can conquer tension without medical help,
Yes, in today's world if you can do all these things, then you are most likely the family dog!

Let's face it; we live in an age of gimmicks and funny sayings. It's a time when forty is the new thirty, when you can shop until you drop, "on line", and when bored middle-class house wives discuss what theme they're having for their Christmas tree this year—and yet for all that, we're still not really happy.

It's a time when we will spend money on absolutely anything that will help us cope with, and enjoy life just a little more. It's the age where stress is the "in" word, and where we will try aromatherapy, reflexology, head massage, yoga, transcendental meditation and even hypnotherapy (to name just a few) in order to feel better. If there's something new out there, we'll certainly pay through the teeth for it, and hope that we've finally found the miracle cure.

If you're looking for peace, a peace that lies inside of yourself, a peace that can't be bought in a shop, found inside in a bottle, or ordered "on-line", then why not try and get to know Jesus?

Enjoy the following true story—*The body of Abraham Lincoln was lying in state. He had been murdered in Washington DC, and his remains were being removed back to Springfield, Illinois.*

Thousands of people lined up to pay their respects. In the queue was a poor black woman, carrying her four-year-old son. When they reached the President's body, the woman lifted her son up in the air and said, "Honey, take a good long look. That man died for you!"

Every one of us could surely point to Jesus and say those self same words, "That man died for you!" Why not make the effort and try and get to know Him this Christmas?

Reflection number 106

LOVE IS TIME

Four brothers left home for college, and after many years of study and hard work they prospered as successful doctors and lawyers.

One evening over dinner they chatted together, discussing the very beautiful and expensive Christmas gifts that they were able to give to their elderly mother who lived far away in another city.

The first son said to his brothers, "I had a huge house built for Mama. I am assured by the builder that she will most certainly spend her twilight days in the lap of luxury."

The second son said, "I spent a hundred thousand pounds on a top of the range Music Theatre for the ground floor of Mama's new house—I know for a fact she will adore it."

Not to be outdone the third son boasted, "Well, after much deliberation I had my Mercedes dealer deliver Mama an SL600—the neighbours will be so jealous."

Finally the fourth son spoke up, "Listen to this boys, you know how Mama used love to read the Bible, and how she isn't feeling all that good with regards to her health at the moment. Well, I met a priest in hospital one day who told me about a parrot that can recite the entire Bible. It took twenty priests twelve years to teach the parrot how to do this. I pledged that I would contribute £100,000 a year for twenty years to his church—I know it sounds frightfully expensive, but it was worth it. Mama just has to name any chapter and verse, and the parrot will recite it." All the brothers were impressed.

After the Christmas holidays Mama sent out her usual thank you notes. She wrote: "John, the house you built is huge. Unfortunately I can only live in one room, but am forced regularly to clean the entire dwelling—Thanks anyway."

"Michael, you built me an expensive Music Theatre with Dolby sound. I believe it can hold 50 people, but sadly all my friends are dead and I have only the cat for company. I've lost my hearing and I'm nearly blind—I'll never use it, but thank you for the gesture just the same."

"Andrew, sadly I am much too old to travel. I stay at home all the time now and have my groceries delivered, so I never get to use the Mercedes you sent. All the same, the thought was very nice—Thank you!"

"Dearest Peter, you were the only son to have the good sense to give a little thought to your gift. The chicken was delicious! Thank you ever so much!"

As we distribute our expensive gifts to our family members and to our friends, lets think also about how we might be able to give them some love this Christmas. Children and old people spell love with four simple letters—"T.I.M.E." **Have you any to spare?**

Reflection number 107

ACQUANTANCES AND FRIENDS

An acquaintance has never seen you cry. A real friend has shoulders soggy from your tears.

An acquaintance doesn't know your parents' first names. A real friend has their phone numbers in his address book.

An acquaintance brings a bottle of wine to your party. A real friend comes early to help you cook, and stays late to help you clean.

An acquaintance hates it when you call after he has gone to bed. A real friend asks you why you took so long to call.

An acquaintance wants to talk with you about your problems. A real friend wants to help you with your problems.

An acquaintance wonders about your romantic history. A real friend could easily blackmail you.

An acquaintance, when visiting, acts like a guest. A real friend opens your refrigerator and helps himself.

An acquaintance thinks the friendship is over when you have an argument. A real friend calls you after you've had a fight.

An acquaintance expects you to always be there for them. A real friend expects to always be there for you!

As we make our resolutions, let's promise that we will be a real friend to those around us, that we will never judge, and that we will try every day to put the commandment of Christ to love our neighbour into practice.

Remember Ecclesiasticus 6:14-15, *"A faithful friend is a sure shelter, whoever finds one has found a rare treasure. A faithful friend is something beyond price, there is no measuring their worth. A faithful friend is the elixir of life, and those who fear the Lord will find one."*

Reflection number 108

FUNNY BUT TRUE

Enjoy!

1. Never, under any circumstances, take a sleeping pill and a laxative on the same night.
2. If you had to identify in one word the reason why the human race has not achieved, and never will achieve its full potential, that word has got to be "meetings".
3. There is a very fine line between "a hobby" and "a mental illness".
4. People who want to share their religious views with you, almost never want you to share yours with them.
5. You should not confuse your career with your life!
6. Nobody cares if you can't dance well—just get up and dance.
7. Never lick a steak knife.
8. The most destructive force in the universe is gossip.
9. You should never say anything to a woman that even remotely suggests that you think she's pregnant, unless you can see an actual baby emerging from her at that moment.
10. There comes a time when you should stop expecting other people to make a big deal about your birthday—that time is age eleven.
11. The one thing that unites all human beings, regardless of age, gender, religion, economic status or ethnic background, is that deep down inside, we all believe that we are above average drivers.
12. A person who is nice to you, but rude to a waiter in a restaurant is not a nice person. (This is very important. Pay attention. It never fails.)
13. "Real friends" love you, no matter what!
14. Never be afraid to try something new. Remember that a lone amateur called Noah built the Ark, and a large group of professionals built the Titanic.

However, if I could add a No. 15 it would be—'*Remember that you personally are made in the image and likeness of God! Try and make a little space in your life for Him every day,* and in every situation you find yourself, ask the following question, "What would Jesus do here, if He were me"?'

Reflection number 109

THE SKY'S THE LIMIT

Last Tuesday, while lounging on the settee watching "Pretty Woman", I exploded with laughter as an unusually nervous Richard Gere tried to chat up a voluptuous Julia Roberts. "What's your name?" he asked her, to which she cooed in reply, "Well Sugar, it's whatever you want it to be!"

While it's a kind of a chic-flic movie, I couldn't help but think that life too can be whatever way we want it to be! Every moment of every day we are faced with choices and decisions, all of which go to make up the consequences of our lives. While we might resort occasionally to becoming players in "the blame game", irresponsibly laying fault at the feet of others, in truth we all write our own life stories, we are all authors of our own destinies. Leaving aside crime, no one can really force us to do what we don't want to do.

There's a lovely story told about a young lad who decided one day that he wanted to become a saint. He had heard at School about a saint called Simon Stylites whose marble statue stood on top of a huge pillar in the centre of the town—this was definitely the saint that he wanted to imitate. Unfortunately for him he had no pillar to perch himself upon, so he decided to modestly made do with a meagre kitchen chair. Sadly within two minutes he was forced to move, as his mother needed to get past him in order to go to the dustbin. Immediately after that his sister needed to get to the fridge which meant moving time again, and when finally his twin brother tried to topple his chair over he decided it was best all round to call sainthood a day, well, on that particular day anyway. As his family laughed and joked about the fact that he had no sticking power, the young lad muttered under his breath, "You don't understand. It's just not possible to become a saint here in this house!"

For all of us, anything is possible, even sainthood for that matter. We can all be whoever we want, or whatever we want. We can be modern day Mother Teresas and real life examples of Jesus Christ to all those around us—it just depends on how serious we are about putting the gospel into practice. Alternatively, we can opt to be dictators, making the lives of all those around us totally miserable and unhappy—examples of both kinds of people are to be found all about us, in our families, our workplaces and in our neighbourhoods.

At the end of the day, the decision is all down to us and no one else. What do you want out of life?

Reflection number IIO

KIDS SAY THE LOVELIEST THINGS

What is love? Saint Paul in his Letter to the Corinthians, tells us that "Love is patient and kind; it is never jealous; love is not boastful or conceited; it is never rude or selfish; it does not take offence, and it is not resentful.

More recently, a group of professional people posed the question, "What does love mean?" to a gathering of children aged between 4 and 8. The answers they got were broader and deeper than anyone could have imagined—I bet they make you smile!

"When my grandmother got arthritis she couldn't bend over and paint her toenails anymore. So my grandfather does it for her all the time, even when his hands have got arthritis too. That's love." Rebecca—age 8

When someone loves you the way they say your name is different. You just know that your name is safe in their mouth." Billy—age 4

"Love is when a girl puts on perfume and a boy puts on aftershave, and they go out and smell each other." Karl—age 5

"Love is when you go out to eat and you give somebody most of your chips without making them give you any of theirs." Chrissy—age 6

"Love is what makes you smile when you're tired." Terri—age 4

"Love is when my mommy makes coffee for my daddy and she takes a sip before giving it to him, to make sure it's not burny." Danny—age 7

"Love is what's in the room with you at Christmas, if you stop opening presents and listen." Bobby—age 7

"Love is when you tell a guy you like his shirt, then he wears it everyday." Noelle—age 7

"During my piano recital I was on a stage and I was scared. I looked at all the people watching me, and then I saw my daddy waving and smiling. He was the only one doing that. I wasn't scared anymore," Cindy—age 8

"*Love is when Mommy gives Daddy the best piece of chicken.*" *Elaine-age 5*

"*Love is when Mommy sees Daddy smelly and sweaty and still says he is handsomer than Robert Redford.*" *Chris—age 7*

"*Love is when your puppy licks your face even after you left him alone all day.*" *Mary Ann—age 4*

"*I know my older sister loves me because she gives me all her old clothes and has to go out and buy new ones.*" *Lauren—age 4*

"*When you love somebody, your eyelashes go up and down and little stars come out of you.*" *Karen—age 7*

And the final one—Author and lecturer Leo Buscaglia once talked about a contest he was asked to judge. The purpose of the contest was to find the most caring child (now this certainly will melt your heart). The winner was a four-year-old child whose next-door neighbour was an elderly man who had recently lost his wife. Upon seeing the man cry, the little boy went into his neighbour's yard, climbed onto the man's lap, and just sat there. When his Mother asked him what he had said to the neighbour, the little boy replied, *"Nothing, I just helped him cry."*

Amazing—isn't it? Children can teach us so much, if we could only take the time to sit down and listen to them!

Reflection number III

I'M WORTH A FORTUNE

At his seminar, a well-known speaker began by holding up a £20.00 note. In a room filled with about 200 people, he asked the question, "Who would like this £20.00?" Hands immediately went up in the air.

"Well", he said, "I'm certainly going to give it to one of you, but first, let me show you something. The speaker proceeded to crumple the £20.00 note up into a ball and then asked, "Who wants it now?" Still, all the hands went up in the air. Well, he laughed, "What if I do this?" and he dropped the £20.00 note onto the ground and began to grind it into the floor with his shoe. By this stage it was both crumpled and dirty—"Now, who still wants it?" he said.

Again all the hands went up into the air. "My friends, we have learned a very valuable lesson", He said. "Note that no matter what I did to the money, you all still wanted it, simply because it did not decrease in value—it was still worth £20.00.

Many times in our lives we are dropped, crumpled, and ground into the dirt by the decisions we make, and the circumstances that come our way. We feel at times as though we are worthless. But no matter what has happened or what will happen, we will never lose our value. Dirty or clean, crumpled or finely creased, we are still priceless to those who truly love us. The worth of our lives comes not in what we do, or who we know, but by who we are! We are special, simply because God made us that way, and no one can ever change that fact!"

Don't ever forget that!

Reflection number 112

LIVING LIFE TO THE FULL

I've always believed that life is for living, and living to the full, and that the greatest commandment of God is to love, not selectively but absolutely. If our faith doesn't encourage us to do this, I suspect we may just be missing the point of what the Gospel is all about.

So often in life we waste our chances, we let fear rule our lives, we think that there will always be a cloud at the end of our tunnel, we let our past and our present totally control our future, and we end up being too cautious and not prepared to cast our nets out into the deep.

In talking to many of my friends who have worked in the same place for twenty years, I often wonder have they really twenty years experience, or simply one years experience multiplied by twenty? So many of them settling for so little over the years, and as time moved on accepting even less—not prepared to take any chances, and tragically not prepared to believe in themselves and the abundant gifts that they have to offer.

Enjoy the reflection—whoever wrote it, fully understood John 10:10.

There are moments in life when you miss someone so much that you just want to pick them out of your dreams and hug them. So, when you want to meet that special person, don't go for looks; they can deceive. Don't go for wealth; even that fades away. Go for someone who makes you smile, because it takes only a smile to make a dark day seem bright—find that someone who will make your heart smile.

Dream what you want to dream; go where you want to go; be what you want to be, because you have only one life and one chance to do all the things you want to do.

May you have enough happiness to make you sweet, enough trials to make you strong, enough sorrow to keep you human and enough hope to make you happy. The happiest of people don't necessarily have the best of everything; they just make the most of everything that comes along their way—they live life as an exclamation, not an explanation.

The brightest future will always be based on a forgotten past; you can't go forward in life until you let go of your past failures and heartaches—we're all human, and because we're human we make mistakes.

When you were born, you were crying and everyone around you was smiling. Live your life so at the end when you go forward to meet God, you're the one who is smiling and everyone around you is crying.

So, don't count the years—count the memories. Life is not measured by the number of breaths we take, but by the moments that take our breath away!

Reflection number 113

THE LORD IS MY PACE SETTER

If you put a buzzard in a pen that is 6 feet by 8 feet and entirely open at the top, the bird, in spite of its ability to fly, will be an absolute prisoner. The reason is that a buzzard always begins a flight from the ground with a run of 10 to 12 feet. Without space to run, as is its habit, it will not even attempt to fly, but will simply remain a prisoner for life in a small jail with no top.

The ordinary bat that flies around at night, a remarkably nimble creature in the air, cannot take off from a level place. If it is placed on the floor or flat ground, all it can do is shuffle about helplessly, until it reaches some slight elevation from which it can throw itself into the air—then, at once, it takes off like a flash.

A bumblebee, if dropped into an open tumbler, will be there until it dies, unless of course it is taken out. It never sees its means of escape right there at the top of the tumbler, but always persists in trying to find some way out through the sides near the bottom. Sadly it will seek a way where none exists, until it completely destroys itself.

In many ways we are like the buzzard, the bat, and the bumblebee. We struggle with problems, worries and frustrations, not ever realizing that the answer is right there . . . "Above us"

In our world today where stress is more common than the common cold, where everyday problems seem to be much bigger and much more severe than ever before, and where we're prepared to try out every kind of expensive therapy and nouveau method of healing that's available, it's sad that God is very often our last port of call, that is if we even call upon Him at all—such a pity that we don't realize what we're missing!

Enjoy the following reflection—it's a re-hash of an old treasure (the 23rd Psalm) that I'm sure we've all heard before, and one that we could well do to pray every day!

The Lord is my pace setter I shall not rush.

He makes me stop for quiet intervals.

He provides me with images of stillness through calmness of mind, His guidance is peace.

Even though I have a great many things to accomplish each day, I will not fret, for His presence is here.

His timelessness, His all importance will keep me in balance.

He prepares refreshment and renewal in the midst of my activity by anointing my head with his oils of tranquillity.

My cup of joyous energy overflows.

Truly harmony and effectiveness shall be the fruits of my hours, for I shall walk in the pace of the Lord, and dwell in His House forever!

Reflection number 114

LOVE ME LITTLE BUT LOVE ME LONG

An elderly Irishman lay dying in his bed. While suffering the agonies of impending death, he suddenly smelled the aroma of his favourite cheese scones wafting up the stairs. He gathered his remaining strength, and lifted himself from the bed.

Leaning against the wall, he slowly made his way out of the bedroom, and with even greater effort, gripping the railing with both hands, he crawled downstairs. With laboured breath, he leaned against the doorframe and gazed into the kitchen. Were it not for death's agony, he would have thought himself already in heaven, for there spread out upon waxed paper on the kitchen table were dozens of his favourite cheese scones. Was it heaven? Or was it one final act of heroic love from his devoted Irish wife of sixty years, seeing to it that he left this world a happy man?

Mustering one great final effort, he threw himself towards the table, landing on his knees in a rumpled posture. With parched lips open, he could almost taste the cheese scone before it was in his mouth, seemingly bringing him back to life. The aged and withered hand trembled on its way to the nearest scone at the edge of the table, when suddenly his hand was smacked angrily with a massive wooden spoon . . . . DON'T EVEN THINK ABOUT IT!!" his wife roared, "they're for the wake!!"

Isn't it amazing that whenever a person dies we're almost ready to canonise them, and yet when that same person was alive, there were times when we would almost begrudge them daylight. There's a lovely old saying in Ireland that goes, "love me little but love me long"—how very powerful!

While on earth Jesus gave us a new commandment, "love one another as I have loved you." Let's be honest about it, there are times for all of us when it's difficult, really difficult to love those around us. It's much easier to throw a few pounds to a local charity or help those in the third world; rather than love the person next door to you who drives you around the bend with their loud music and their smelly mutt of a dog who runs after your car wheels every morning. Likewise, signing a petition against racism for Amnesty International is certainly less draining on the emotions than sorting out a family disagreement where brother and sister haven't spoken for ten years.

The reality is that we are called to start our love with those we live with and live beside, hard as that may seem. However, while our love starts there, let's remember that it doesn't have to end there!

Reflection number 115

GOOD OLD NOAH

Some people are filled with anger. The result is that life for them is miserable and wretched, and to make matters worse they depress everyone they come in contact with—we immediately want to cross the street and avoid them as soon as we see them coming. Sadly these people are to be pitied, because they really have missed out on the message of Christ—"Peace I leave with you. My own peace I give you". (John 14:27)

Christ never promised us that life was ever going to be a bed of roses, a perpetual honeymoon, or everything our own way, but he did promise us that he would be with us until the end of time. The peace he offers us is not an escape from the everyday realities of sickness, poverty or family troubles—it is a peace of conquest, that with His help we can overcome all the trials and troubles that come our way as part of life. However first and foremost, to obtain Christ's help, we have to chill out, speak with Him regularly, and admit that we are nothing without Him.

Enjoy the reflection—it's called Noah's beatitudes. And if it could work for poor old Noah, who I'm sure at times wondered what was happening, then surely it can work for us too.

1) Don't miss the boat. 2) Remember that we are all in the same boat—we all have our own personal struggles. 3) Plan ahead. It's worth noting that it wasn't raining when Noah built the Ark. 4) Stay fit. When you're 600 years old God may still ask you to do something big. 5) Don't listen to people who criticise and who do damage with their big mouths (I secretly suspect that poor old Noah may have had to keep those nasty woodpeckers locked away in a secret cage), just get on with the job that God wants to be done. 6) Build your future on high ground. 7) For safety's sake, travel in pairs. 8) Speed isn't always an advantage—remember that the snails were on board with the cheetahs. 9) When you're stressed, float around for a while. 10) Remember that the Ark was built by an amateur and the Titanic was built by professionals. 11) And finally, keep in mind that no matter how bad the storm is for you, whenever you're travelling with God, there's always a rainbow waiting somewhere around the corner!

Reflection number 116

FEELING CRUCIFIED

Good Friday is the day when Christians around the world stop and remember the Passion and Crucifixion of Jesus!

One of the many ways our Church re-visits Good Friday is to gather together in prayer and reflection upon the journey of Jesus to the Cross. Let me introduce to you a modern interpretation of the Ninth Station, where Jesus falls for the third time—because we're all human, and let's be honest about it, we all fall; it's one station that many of us can identify with.

"Michael had always feared that it would end like this. No one realised the terrible pressure that he suffered during his final year at school—it was a constant struggle. His parents were so proud when his results paved the way for a university scholarship. He will never forget the journey from his home to the university town. While it wasn't said, he knows his father was recapturing missed opportunities from his own life. Now the notice board tells him that he has failed—and not for the first time—these were his repeats. Maybe he should get away. He has a friend in London . . . or is it Manchester?

Dear Lord, this Station demands that we feel the pain of this young man. There are some who would say that he could have done better, but only he himself knows the real truth of the situation. May he and all who feel so weighed down and worried find strength in that great story you told . . . 'a certain man had two sons'. We pray for Michael and for all who are like him, that having come to their senses, they too may feel the Father's embrace, even though they might yet be a 'long way off.'"

It's hard today for young people, and for parents (who were young people just yesterday). As the Ninth Station was all about understanding and loving our young people, I enclose the following wee prayer for their parents.

Lord God I am afraid to let them go, and yet I know I must. I taught them as best I could when they were helpless and dependant upon me, but now they are on their own—it frightens me to realise that they do not think as I think. Oddly enough, that's an answer to my prayer, because I have always tried to encourage my children to develop as individuals, but in truth, facing the fruits of one's convictions is frightening. Lord, deep down I long to be with them and protect them in this difficult world with all its problems and temptations.

Lord, be their inspiration and guide them on the stony path through life. Preserve them from sin. Protect them from evil. You gave your beloved disciple John into the care of your Mother when he was but a youth. Oh please do the same for my children.

Dearest Mary, you have been a mother to me. Be a mother to them. Make up for what is lacking in me as a parent. Love them and guide them and lead them in the way of truth. May they be filled with your Holy Spirit, and may I be filled with the courage to stand back and let them go, Amen.

Reflection number 117

SLOWING DOWN

Thank God the month of May has arrived. It's so great to see the nights getting longer, the leaves coming out on the trees and holidays from school and work just around the corner. Such a pity though that so many of us don't take the time to stop and just enjoy it. Sadly, we all seem to be in such a rush, although God only knows to where. We delude ourselves that we're important, and that work, or home for that matter, could never go on without us—how foolish are we? Every day we try to make deadlines, earn more money, build bigger houses, drive faster cars and visit more exotic countries—such a pity we just can't stop and enjoy what we have, instead of always wanting something else. It's worth noting that our cemeteries hold the remains of some of our loved ones who never found the time to stop, and who thought that they somehow couldn't be done without—how wrong were they!

Enjoy the reflection—hope it helps you to slow down! After September 11th, a company invited the remaining members of other companies whose offices had been decimated by the attack on the Twin Towers to come and share their new office space. After getting to know the new people around him, a head of security wrote down the following stories as to why these people were alive.

"On September 11th the Chairman of the company got in late that day because his son started Nursery School. Another man was alive because it was his turn to bring in the donuts. One woman was late because her alarm clock didn't go off in time. One was late because of a car accident, which meant the traffic was tailed back for a long way. Another missed his bus. One woman spilled food on her clothes that morning and had to take time to change. Another woman's car wouldn't start. One went back to answer the telephone. One had a child that dawdled and didn't get ready as soon as he should have (both she and her husband scolded the child that morning for keeping them late). One couldn't get a taxi. Another man wore a new pair of shoes, but before he arrived at work he developed a blister on his foot and stopped at a chemist to buy a Band-Aid, and that is simply why he is alive today."

Now when I'm stuck in traffic, miss an elevator, turn back to answer a ringing telephone (all the little things that annoy us) I think to myself, this is exactly where I'm supposed to be at this very moment.

Next time your morning seems to be going wrong, the children are slow about getting dressed, you can't seem to find the car keys, you hit every traffic light, don't get mad or frustrated; remember that someone is watching over you—when God made time, he made plenty of it!

Reflection number 118

LILY THE PINK

I celebrated the Funeral Mass last Tuesday of one the most beautiful people to ever grace this earth. Lily Lennon, or "Lily the pink" as I affectionately called her at times, was still young at heart at the grand old age of 101. She was a joy to attend each month, an absolute lady filled with a love for life and all that it held, sitting waiting for me every first Friday, dressed in her finest regalia with her hair styled to perfection.

Lily had been through the wars, and definitely had the tee shirt to prove it. She has witnessed the death of her husband, her only son, her son in law as well as two of her grand daughters, and still for all that she carried no bitterness or anger—her faith in God strong as a rock, and her belief in the Resurrection unshakable!

Apart from being the only person I have ever known to reach "the ton", she was also the only person I have ever heard of to take their first sip of alcohol at 97.

At 98 she explained to me that her daughter left the landing light on each night, just in case she felt that she needed to use the bathroom. When I asked was she able to get up and go to the WC without any attendance, she looked me in the eye and said, "Of course. Why do you ask that? Do you think there's something wrong with me?"

That was the thing about Lily, she never failed to both shock and delight you, her body may have slowed up towards the end, but her mind remained sharp as a cut-throat razor.

I learned so much from Lily. Hand on heart I can say, "My life is all the richer for having known her". She understood fully the words of Jesus in John's gospel when he said, "I came that you would have life, and life to the full".

Enjoy the reflection. It's called, "Age is a quality of mind". We might ask ourselves after we read it, are we old, or are we truly young at heart?

If you have left your dreams behind, if hope is cold, if you no longer plan ahead, if your ambitions all are dead, then you are old.

But if you make of life the best, and in your life you still have zest, if love you hold, no matter how the years go by, no matter how the birthdays fly—you are not old!

Reflection number 119

CANCER

Cancer has no respect for age, colour or creed—or indeed anyone's feelings for that matter. Cancer is not a nice word. It's a word that makes us put our hands up to our mouths when we hear its name mentioned. Cancer is an illness that has almost certainly hit someone we know—a family member, a friend, a neighbour or a work colleague. There are two very profound points to be made about it. 1. We can live with cancer. 2. We can die with cancer.

A friend of mine Marie Auden (R.I.P.) gave me the following reflection while she was in the middle of her chemotherapy. I can understand why it meant so much to her—She was a very special person indeed, a woman with beauty and hope drawn all over her face, despite the personal suffering that she must have endured. Whenever I looked at her in Church I could always see the face of the Good Samaritan from Luke's Gospel, you just knew that she always had time to stop, to listen and to help her neighbour.

"Cancer is so limited . . . Why? Well, it cannot cripple love, it cannot shatter hope, it cannot corrode faith, and it cannot eat away peace. Cancer cannot destroy confidence, it cannot kill friendship, it cannot shut out memories and it cannot silence courage. It can never invade the soul, it cannot reduce eternal life and it cannot quench the spirit. Cancer cannot lessen the power of the Resurrection!"

God bless all who have cancer, care for those who have cancer, pray for those who have cancer and raise money for those who have cancer. It's important to remember that we're all called to do something to help, big or small. Christ doesn't want watery passive spectators as His followers.

Mother Teresa said, "At the end of the day we will not be judged by how many diplomas we have received, how much money we have made, or how many great things we have done. We will be judged by, 'I was hungry and you gave me to eat, I was naked and you clothed me, I was sick and you visited me, I was homeless and you took me in.'"

Let's open our eyes, Christ is all around us in a distressing disguise—it's not enough to feel sorry for the sick—we have to do something to help!

Reflection number 120

STOP THE WORLD AND LET ME OFF

'Relax—take a chill pill', is an expression that is commonly used by our young people. We can learn a lot from the 'teeny-boppers', after all, it's good to 'chill', to take time out, to de-stress, to occasionally say 'No' back to them, like they say it to us. Coronary Care has its fair share of patients who need to 'chill', that is, if they're going to survive the pace. And, let's face it, our cemeteries have headstones erected to all those who never quite learned to 'chill' in time.

The following is the prayer of a tired mother who needs to 'chill'. Think you can identify with it?

Lord, Lord! Have they all forgotten?
*   I am a person!*
*   I may be a mother and a wife,*
*   but I am also a person.*
I feel as if I am taken for granted and used.
Someone is always coming at me with a need:
*   a runny nose,*
*   a hungry stomach,*
*   a difficult school assignment,*
*   a paper to be typed,*
*   a quarrel to be settled.*
*   Sometimes I want to scream, 'Leave me alone!'*
I need someone to care about me, Lord.
*   I need to have someone hear 'me' tell about 'my' day.*
*   I need an occasional compliment*
*   or a night out.*
I need some quiet Lord—
*   my ears are jangling with family noise.*

I need time: to read a book that I enjoy, to look out the window at the sky, to think without interruption. I need time to be 'me'—the me that was born with my own identity, the me that used to have her own first name, the me that would still like to learn and change.

Help me Lord, to coordinate my need and their needs. Help me to teach my children that part of growing up is respecting other people's needs for privacy and attention, and that I am most certainly one of those 'other' people!

While we may never be able to change those around us, we can most certainly change ourselves, and the way in which we live our lives. It's never too late to make changes—life is all about choices. My advice is, every day; take some time to 'chill'. The Gospel tells us that even Jesus went to a quiet place to be by himself, and to pray. So, if is was good enough for the Saviour of the world, then surely it's got to be good for us too!

Reflection number 121

HELP ME SEE THE WHOLE PERSON

Failure to love one's neighbour, I believe, is the greatest failure for a Christian. Often however, it is not even seen as a sin.

All of us have a great capacity to love, but sadly we don't use it enough, we don't make the effort, we're content to hold onto bitterness, anger and even hate.

The actor Christopher Reeve was famous for his portrayal of Superman in the movies. However, as a result of a fall from a horse he ended up in a wheelchair, paralysed from the neck down. After his accident he received 100,000 letters of sympathy and support from well-wishers, which led him to ask, "Why does it take a tragedy before we show our appreciation and love for one another?"

All too often we leave it too late to show our love and care to the people around us. We leave it too late to mend a quarrel, too late to enjoy our health, too late to enjoy the gift of our children and the gift of our parents—we're so busy doing things that add up to nothing, or holding on to grudges and resentment from way back. Why do we have to wait until a death occurs before we make the effort to stretch out our hand in friendship?

Enjoy the reflection, but let's also try and put it into practice.

God grant us all a wider view
so we might see people's faults through the eyes of **YOU***.*
Teach us not to judge with hasty tongue,
either the **ADULT** *or the* **YOUNG***.*
Give us patience and grace to endure
and of course a stronger faith so we can feel secure.
And instead of remembering, help us Lord to forget
those irritations that sometimes cause us to fret.

Help us to offer a friendly, helping hand
and try in all ways to understand
because **ALL OF US** *whoever we*
are are trying to reach "that unreachable star".
For the **GREAT** *and* **SMALL** . . . *the* **GOOD** *and* **BAD***,*
the **YOUNG** *and* **OLD** . . . *the* **SAD** *and* **GLAD**
are asking today, **IS LIFE WORTH LIVING?**
and your answer Lord is in **LOVING** *and* **GIVING.**
For only love can make us kind
And **KINDNESS** *of* **HEART** *brings* **PEACE** *of* **MIND***.*
So by giving love let us start each day
to lift the clouds of **HATE** *and* **FEAR** *away.*

Reflection number 122

HELL HATH NO FURY . . .

Enjoy the story—I'm told it's true.

After 17 years of marriage, a man dumped his lovely wife for his young secretary. His new Barbie doll girlfriend demanded that she wanted to live in the couple's multimillion-dollar home, and since the man's lawyers were the best that money could possibly buy, he won. He gave his now ex-wife just 3 days to move out.

The poor woman spent the first day packing her belongings into boxes, crates and suitcases. On the second day, she had the removal men call and collect her things. On the third day, she sat down for the last time at their beautiful dining room table by candlelight, listened to some soft background music, and feasted on a pound of shrimp, a jar of caviar, and a bottle of Chardonnay. When she had finished, she went into each room and deposited a few half-eaten shrimp shells, dipped in caviar, into the hollow of the brass curtain rods. She then cleaned up the kitchen and left.

When the husband returned with his new girlfriend, all was bliss for the first few days. Then slowly, the house began to smell. They tried everything; cleaning and mopping and airing the place out. Vents were checked for dead rodents, and carpets were steam cleaned—air fresheners were placed everywhere. Exterminators were brought in to set off gas canisters, during which the happy couple had to move out for a few days—in the end they even paid to replace the expensive wool carpeting, but nothing worked. People stopped coming over to visit. Repairmen refused to work in the house. The maid quit. Finally, they could not take the stench any longer and decided to move.

A month later, even though they had cut their price in half, they could not find a buyer for their stinky house—word had definitely got around.

Finally, they had to borrow a huge sum of money from the bank to purchase a new place.

The ex-wife called her husband, and asked how things were going. He told her the saga of the rotting house. She listened politely, and said that she missed her old home terribly, and would be willing to reduce her divorce settlement in exchange for getting her old home back.

Knowing his ex-wife had no idea how bad the smell was, he agreed on a price that was about one tenth of what the house had been worth, but only on the condition that she sign the papers that very same day. She agreed, and within an hour, his lawyers had everything sorted out.

A week later, the man and his new girlfriend stood smirking as they watched the removal company pack everything to take to their new home. They even packed the expensive brass curtain rods, which were a parting gift from the man's ex-wife, just to show that there were no hard feelings! I love a happy ending, don't you???

Today we might look at both the hurts and the hates that we need to let go of. With proper help (*and believe me it's worth getting—I know from experience*) we can heal ourselves of old wounds, rid ourselves of old injuries, and let go of old grudges that we have been harbouring for years.

We only get one go at life—why go through it crippled with anger?

Reflection number 123

AN UNWISE INVESTMENT

As the summer holidays from school begin, and our children at times almost drive us around the bend, let's think about the following reflection—it's called "family".

I bumped into a stranger as he passed by, "Oh, excuse me please" was my reply. He said, "Please, excuse me too; I also wasn't watching for you." We were very polite, this stranger and I. We went on our way and we said good-bye.

But at home a different story is told, how we treat our loved ones, young and old. Later that day, while cooking the evening meal, my son stood beside me very still. When I turned, I nearly knocked him down. "Move out of the way," I said with a frown. He walked away, his little heart broken. I didn't realise how harshly I'd spoken.

While I lay awake in bed, God's voice came to me and said, "While dealing with a stranger, common courtesy you use, but the family you love, you seem to abuse. Go and look on the kitchen floor, you'll find some flowers there by the door. Those are the flowers he brought for you. He picked them himself: pink, yellow and blue. He stood very quietly not to spoil the surprise, you never saw the tears that filled his little eyes."

By this time, I felt very small, and at this stage my tears began to fall. I quietly went and knelt by his bed; "Wake up, little one, wake up," I said. "Are these the flowers you picked for me?" He smiled, "I found them, out by the tree. I picked them because they're pretty, like you. I knew you'd like them, especially the ones that are blue."

I said, "Son, I'm very sorry for the way I acted today; I shouldn't have yelled at you in that way." He said, "Ach Mammy, that's okay. Sure you know I love you anyway." I said, "Son, I love you too, and I do like the flowers, especially the ones that are blue."

If we died tomorrow, the company that we work for would probably replace us within days, however the family we leave behind will feel their loss for the rest of their lives. Often we commit ourselves more to our work than our family—an unwise investment, don't you think?

Reflection number 124

THE BICYCLE RIDE

Enjoy the story—*At first, I saw God as my observer, my judge, keeping account of all the things I did wrong, working out whether I would go to heaven or hell when I die. He was way out there in the distance, like some sort of President or Prime Minister. I recognised His picture on the wall when I saw it, but I didn't really know Him, not personally anyway.*

However, later on when I met Christ, it seemed as if life was just like a bicycle ride, a tandem bicycle—Christ was at the back, helping me pedal. One day, I can't remember exactly when, He suggested we change places—life has not been the same since.

When I had control, I knew the way—it was boring and predictable; for me it was always working out the shortest distance between two points. But when Jesus took the lead, He knew delightful journeys, up mountains, and through rocky places, all at breakneck speed. At times it was all I could do just to hang on.

Even though at times it felt like madness, He kept saying to me, "Pedal." I worried, and I was anxious, and I asked Him, "Lord, where are you taking me?" He laughed and didn't answer—I learned to trust Him completely. I forgot my boring life and entered fully into the adventure. When I'd say, "I'm scared Lord," He'd lean back and touch my hand. I gained love, peace, acceptance and joy; gifts to take on my journey, my Lord's and mine.

Once day He said, "Give your gifts away. They're extra baggage, too much weight." So I did. I gave them to all the people we met along the way, and I found that in giving I received, and still my burden was light. To be really honest I didn't fully trust Him at first with total control of my life—I was always used to having the control. I liked power. I thought perhaps He might wreck it; but He knows real bicycle secrets, He knows how to make our tandem bend to take sharp corners, He knows how to jump high so that we can clear rocks, and He knows how to fly, so that we can shorten those scary journeys.

I'm learning to stay quiet and pedal in the strangest places, and I'm beginning to enjoy the view and the cool breeze on my face with my constant companion, Jesus Christ. And when I'm sure I just can't do it anymore, He just smiles and says . . . "Pedal! Sure you know I'm never going to leave you on your own!"

Reflection number 125

WHY GOD CREATED CHILDREN

Well, the summer holidays are now in full swing. To those of you who have children around you, whether they are your own, your grandchildren, or your nieces or nephews, here's a wee reflection that will help make you smile.

Whenever your children are out of control, take comfort from the thought that even God's influence did not even extend to His children.

After creating heaven and earth, God created Adam and Eve. Believe it or not, we're told that one of the first things God said to them was "DON'T!"

"Don't what?" Adam replied. "Don't eat the forbidden fruit." God said. "Forbidden fruit? We have forbidden fruit? Hey Eve . . . we have forbidden fruit!!!!!" "No way", said Eve. "Yes, way!" said Adam.

"Do NOT eat the fruit!" said God. "Why?" asked Adam. "Because I am your Father and I said so!" God replied, wondering at that moment why He hadn't stopped His creation after making the elephants. A few minutes later, God saw His children having an apple break in His garden and boy was He mad!

"Didn't I tell you not to eat the fruit?" God asked. "Sure," Adam replied. "Then why did you?" said the Father. "I don't know," said Eve. "She started it!" Adam said. "Did not!" "Did too!" "DID NOT!" Having had it with the two of them, it's obvious that God's punishment was that Adam and Eve should have children of their own. Thus the pattern was set and it has never changed.

However, there is reassurance in the story—if you have persistently and lovingly tried to give your children wisdom and they haven't taken it, don't be too hard on yourself. If God had trouble raising children, what makes you think it would be a piece of cake for you?

THINGS TO THINK ABOUT

1 *You spend the first two years of their life teaching your children to walk and talk. Then you spend the next sixteen telling them to sit down and be quiet.*
2 *Grandchildren are actually God's reward for not killing your own children.*
3 *Parents of teenagers now know why some animals eat their young.*
4 *Children seldom misquote you. In fact, they usually repeat word for word what you shouldn't have said.*
5 *The main purpose of holding children's parties is to remind yourself that there are other children out there; who are actually bolder than yours.*

However, be nice to your kids. Remember that one day they will choose what nursing home you go to. And finally: If you find yourself suffering from a lot of tension and stress because of the summer holidays from school, and you seem to have a constant headache, simply do what it says on the Aspirin bottle: "take two tablets" and "keep away from children."

Reflection number 126

MOTHER

A young mother (whose children I believe regularly drive her to distraction) gave me the following reflection. Hopefully, as we read our way through it we'll understand just how many sacrifices mothers really make, and how they epitomise unconditional love. You could say that they're a just like Christ—don't you think?

The young mother set her foot on the path of life. "Is this a long way?" she asked. The guide replied, "Yes, and it's also a hard way. You will be old before you reach the end of it, but remember that the end will be better than the beginning."

The young mother was happy, she could not believe that anything could be better than these years. Everyday she played with her children. She fed them and bathed them, she taught them how to tie their shoes and ride a bike, she reminded them to feed the dog, do their homework and brush their teeth. The sun shone on them, and the young mother cried aloud to God, "Nothing will ever be lovelier than this."

The night came, and with night came a storm. The path was sometimes dark, and the children shook with fear and cold, but the mother drew them close and covered them with her arms. The children said, "Mother, we are not afraid, for you are near, and no harm can come." The morning came and there was a hill ahead, the children climbed and grew weary, their mother too was weary, but at all times she said to her children, "A little patience and we are there."

The children climbed, and as they climbed they learned to weather the storms of life. With her experience she gave them strength to face the world. Year after year, she showed them compassion, understanding and hope, but most of all she gave them unconditional love. When they reached the top they said, "Mother, we could not have done it without you."

As time went by the mother grew old. She became smaller and weaker. Her children now were tall and strong and they walked with courage. When the mother lay down at night she looked up at the stars and said, "This is a better day than the last, for my children have learned so much and they are now passing these traits on to their children."

When the way became rough for her, the children lifted their mother and gave her their strength, just as she had given them hers. One day they came to a hill, and beyond the hill there was a shining road with golden gates flung wide open. The mother said: "I have reached the end of my journey. Now I know that the end is better than the beginning, for my children can walk with dignity and pride, with their heads held high, and so can their children after them." The children said, "You will always walk with us, Mother, even when you have gone through the gates."

They stood together and watched her, as she went through the golden gates alone. They said: "Even though we cannot see her, she is with us still. A mother like ours is more than a memory, she is a living presence."

Your mother is always with you. She is the whisper of the leaves as you walk down the street and the smell of certain foods that you remember. She is the cool hand on your brow when you're not feeling well; the sound of the rain that lulls you to sleep and she is the colours in the rainbow. Your mother is your birthday morning.

Your mother lives inside your laughter. She is crystallised in every teardrop. A mother shows every emotion—happiness, sadness, fear, jealousy, love, hate, anger, helplessness, excitement, joy and sorrow. She is the place you came from—your first home, she's the map you follow with every step you take. She is your first love; your first friend, even your first enemy. Nothing can separate you, not time, not space . . . . not even death!

Reflection number 127

PRAYER

A priest died and made his way up to the Pearly Gates. Ahead of him in the queue stood an overweight man wearing sunglasses, an extremely loud shirt, a scruffy leather jacket, ripped jeans and busted gutties.

Saint Peter nodded at the man as he stood there in his sloppy attire. "Who are you?" he asked, "so that I may know whether or not I should admit you into heaven." The man replied, "Sir, I'm Jack Thomas junior, taxi-driver, of Noo Yawk City." Saint Peter consulted his list. After a matter of seconds he said to the taxi-driver, "Take a silken robe and a golden staff, and enter the Kingdom of Heaven." The taxi-driver floated into heaven, majestically clothed in his new robe and heavily armed with golden staff.

It was now the priest's turn. He stood tall in his black suit and boomed out, "I am Joseph Snow. I have been parish priest of Saint Mary's Church, for the last forty-three years." Saint Peter once again consulted his list, and after a few moments he said to the priest, "Take a cotton robe and a wooden staff and enter the Kingdom of Heaven."

"Just a cotton-picking minute," the priest said, "if you'll excuse the pun, that is. That man before me was a taxi-driver, and he got a silken robe and a golden staff. How did you work that out?"

Saint Peter paused, looked lovingly into the priest's eyes and said, "Well Father, you know up here in heaven we work by results. The reality is, when you preached, people actually slept. But when Jack drove, people definitely prayed.

In the Gospel the disciples asked Jesus to teach them how to pray. It's not cool today to say that we pray, or that we have faith, or that we go to Church for that matter. It's much more "in" to "kick" religion and religious beliefs, or to boast about the fact that we don't practice or believe in such "hocus pocus".

One thing is certain about prayer—the less we do, the harder it becomes. Maybe one of the reasons why many people find it difficult to pray is not because it's out of tune with the times we live in, but because we've lost the knack of how to pray. We've stopped praying and we don't know how to start again—we don't know how to make contact with God.

To get the skill of how to pray we need two things—a time and a place. It's important to switch off from all the distractions around us and just concentrate. It's worth noting that there are many beautiful little prayer guides, leaflets, tapes and books available today to help us.

Whilst everything we ask for in prayer is never going to come our way, prayer can give us something that we can never get anywhere else, and that's inner peace. Why not give it a go? All the best doctors recommend it—it's very therapeutic, and believe me, the peace that it gives can't be bought anywhere else.

In my prayers I asked God for strength that I might achieve; I was made weak that I might learn humbly to obey. I asked for help that I might do great things; I was given infirmity that I might do better things. I asked for riches that I might be happy; I was given poverty that I might be wise. I asked for all things that I might enjoy life; I was given life that I might enjoy all things. I was given nothing that I asked for; but everything that I hoped for. Despite myself, my prayers were answered; I am among all people most richly blessed!

Reflection number 128

THE FINAL DESTINATION

A couple from New York decided to travel down to Florida in an effort to thaw out during a particularly icy winter. Being total romantics they planned to stay at the very same hotel where they spent their honeymoon 20 years earlier. Because of hectic work schedules and commitments it was impossible to coordinate their travel schedules on the same day, and so the husband left New York and flew to Florida on Thursday, with his wife flying down the following day.

The husband checked into the hotel. His room boasted a top of the range computer and so he decided to send an e-mail to his wife. However, while typing he accidentally left out one letter in her e-mail address, and without realising his error, he sent the e-mail.

Meanwhile, somewhere in Houston, a very sad and lonely widow returned home from her husband's funeral. He had been a minister for many years and was "called home to glory", following a very sudden and unexpected heart attack. The widow decided to check her e-mail expecting to find messages of sympathy from relatives and friends. After reading the first message, she fainted. Her son rushed into the room when he heard the thud and found his mother sprawled out on the floor. When he looked at the computer screen this is what he read:

"To: My Loving Wife.
Subject: I've arrived!
Date: 16 January 2004
I know you're surprised to hear from me. Believe it or not they have computers here, and you are now allowed to send e-mails to your loved ones. I've just made it, and have been checked in. I see to my great delight that everything has been prepared for your arrival tomorrow. Looking forward to seeing you then.
P.S. It sure is hot down here!"

Wherever we get to on the last day, there's one thing for sure, there will be no mistake in the address we're sent to. Let's make sure that the way we live, and the ways in which we treat those around us, are Christs ways. Otherwise, we may just find that our final destination might be too hot for us!

Reflection number 129

FUNNY HA HA OR FUNNY PECULIAR?

Funny how simple it is for people to trash God and Christian beliefs and then wonder why the world is in the condition it is today.

Funny how we can so easily believe what the newspapers say, but question what the Bible says.

Funny how everyone wants to go to heaven, provided they don't have to believe, think, say, or do anything that the bible asks us. Funny, or should that be scary?

Funny how easily we can say "'I believe in God" but still follow Satan (who by the way also believes in God).

Funny how you can receive a joke in your e-mail and you immediately want to pass it on to all your friends in your address book, but when you receive a message regarding the Lord, you think twice about passing it on.

Funny how many people boast about not going to Church; or about how the Church and its teachings are outdated, and yet they still want to be married in Church, have their kids baptised in Church, receive everything the Church has to offer, and eventually when life is complete have their funeral service in a Church—funny that!

Funny how the lewd, crude, vulgar and obscene messages pass freely through cyberspace, but the public discussion of Jesus is suppressed in some schools and many work places. Funny, isn't it?

Funny how someone can be so fired up for Christ on Sunday, but be an invisible Christian the rest of the week.

Funny how I can be more worried about what other people think of me than what God thinks of me.

However, funny as it all may be, can you hear anyone laughing? I can't!

Reflection number 130

SHOPPING FOR HUSBANDS

A new "Husband Super Store" opened where women could choose a spouse from among the many varieties of men on offer. Each floor boasted a department that displayed hunky men with positive attributes.

Inside a basic rule applied, once women entered a particular floor to view the talent on offer, they were not permitted to retrace their steps and select someone from a previous department. There was to be no running back and forward, no contrasting, and no comparing the many men on offer—it was purchase on the spot, or move on. A couple of girlfriends travelled to the "Husband Store" looking for their ideal man. Inside the building this is what they discovered.

Ground floor—The entrance here had a sign that read, "The men in this area have jobs and love kids." The women read the sign and said, "Well, that's better than not having a job or not loving kids, but I wonder what's further up?" So, up they quickly travelled.

On the first floor the sign read, "These men have high paying jobs, love kids, and are extremely good looking." "Hmmm," said the ladies, "Good stuff. But I wonder what's up above?"

The Second floor sign read, "These men have high paying jobs, are extremely good looking, love kids and help with the housework." "Wow," said the women, "Very tempting indeed." However, since there was another floor they hastily climbed.

The third floor—This sign on this door read, "These men have high paying jobs, love kids, are extremely good looking, help with the housework and have a very strong romantic streak." "Oh, mercy me," the women cried, "This is a dream come true!" "Hold on a minute", one of the women cried, "If the men are getting better with every floor we climb, just imagine what's waiting for us on the final floor!" So, up to the fourth floor they all raced.

At the entrance to the fourth floor the sign read, "This floor is empty and exists only to prove that women are impossible to please! The exit to this building is to your left; please try not to fall down the stairs as you leave—you understand that the many eligible men you passed by will obviously be in no rush to help you!"

On a serious note, there are some of us who just cannot be pleased. No matter what we have, we want more, always hoping that latest thing on the market, the newest fad, the hottest gadget will manage to fill that gap—and yet it never does! We're constantly found wanting. We want to meet that special person, then we want to be engaged, then we want to be married and then we want a family. And while we're in the process of getting all of this, we also want a fabulous home, a new car, designer clothes and foreign holidays. It's no wonder so many relationships fail—we spend so much of our time wanting, and so very little appreciating and simply enjoying.

When giving advice old people used to say, "Count your blessings". Perhaps if we tried that today, instead of constantly wanting more, there might be a whole lot more contentment in our lives!

Reflection number 131

GOD'S MESSAGE TO YOU

Singers are always telling us through their songs just how much they love that special person in their lives. Enjoy the following reflection—the words are more beautiful than the lyrics of any love song. Simply slip your name in where you see the dots, and realise just how special you are to God.

This is God's message to you
I made you . . . . in my own image and likeness,
and when I made you I saw that you were good.

Before the world was made . . . . I chose you,
chose you in Christ, to be holy and spotless,
and to live in love in my presence.

I chose you . . . . to live with me, you . . . . are my friend.
Do not be afraid . . . . for I have saved you.
I have called you by your name . . . .

When you go through deep waters and great trouble,
I will be with you.
When you go through rivers of difficulty, you will not drown.
When you go through the fire of suffering
you will not be burned up—the flame will not destroy you.
Do not be afraid . . . . for I am with you.

You are precious in my eyes . . . .
You are honoured and I love you.
You are always in my presence . . . .
and I hold you by you right hand.

Now I will guide you with advice,
and in the end receive you into glory.

Christ is in you . . . . , your hope in glory!

Reflection number 132

THE PUPIL'S PRAYER

The summer holidays are now over. The once brand new school uniforms already look as if they're well and truly broken in, young people are even talking about coursework for exams, and sadly our September days are becoming all too short as we coast our way along into Autumn.

There's something about a new academic year that always makes me feel so sorry for children. It's not as if I had some horrendous experience at school—in fact school was lovely. It's just that I can still smell that stomach-wrenching smell that so brazenly wafted up your nostrils as soon as you entered the foyer on that first grey Monday in September—that awful smell that smelt something like popcorn and bubblegum rubbed around together on the bottom of a leather-soled shoe. Even thinking about it today still makes me want to heave.

It's important to pray for our children, constantly. God keep them safe from harm and danger, sickness and accident, bullies and strangers, and let's not forget paedophiles and murderers—let's face it, they definitely exist.

Below is a prayer that was given to me for children and young people. It's called "The Pupil's Prayer". My prayer for them is simply that their schooldays may fly, and may each and every one of them be filled with laughter and happiness.

O Lord Jesus, be with me all through today, and help me to live as I ought to live. Be with me in my lessons so that I may never give up on any task. No matter how hard or difficult lessons may be, help me to master whatever comes my way.

Be with me at my games, so that whether I win or lose, I may play fair. I pray that if I win, I may not boast, and if I lose, I may not make excuses.

Be with me in my pleasure, so that I may never find pleasure in anything I would afterwards regret, or in anything I would not like You or my parents to see me do.

Be with me in my home so that I may be kind and considerate, and that I may try to make the work of those around me easier, and not harder.

Be with me on the streets, so that I may give credit to my school, to those who love me, and of course to myself.

Help me Lord to be the kind of person You want me to be, Amen.

Reflection number 133

DON'T MESS WITH WOMEN

A young woman and a middle-aged man were involved in a horrific car accident. Both vehicles were completely destroyed, but thankfully neither of the drivers were hurt. As they stood there together on the side of the road surveying the damage, the young woman took the man by the hand, looked into his eyes, and tearfully said, "Thank God no one is hurt or injured. This must surely be a sign from our Father above that we should be friends". Flattered, and overcome with emotion, the man replied, "Oh yes, I agree with you totally, this is most definitely a sign from God!" The woman sobbed and continued, "And look at this, here's another miracle. My car is completely written off, but this bottle of wine that was sitting here on my passenger seat, it didn't even break. Surely God wants us to drink this wine and celebrate our good fortune—don't you agree?"

The man nodded his head, joyfully opened the bottle and drank half of it. Afterwards he handed the bottle to the woman who took it and fixed the top on securely.

The man noticed the woman shaking, so he put his arm around her shoulder to comfort her, and said, "I thought we were celebrating the fact that no one's hurt. Aren't you having any?" To which the woman replied, "No! Definitely not! I'd rather wait for the police to arrive!"

The moral of the story: Women are clever, crafty and always one step ahead of the posse—don't ever mess with them!

All joking aside, loving one's neighbour can at times be very difficult—especially if it's someone who's constantly on the make, cute as a bag of monkeys and cunning as a fox. Loving the starving in the Sudan, sending money off to the foreign missions and supporting the Hospice are significantly easier alternatives; they don't require as much emotional effort, and are certainly much simpler than having to be nice to some "desperado" who we know for a fact has pulled the wool over our eyes in the past.

Christ sometimes mixed with the strangest of people while on earth—characters that good Church going people wouldn't have walked on the same side of the road as. Christ never ever wrote anyone off, and by loving all those that society classed as "rogues"; He made them feel wanted, needed and special, and by befriending them He showed them how to live another way, a better way.

We will never achieve anything positive or life giving by holding grudges or by judging anyone. The call of the Gospel is to love our neighbour, and sometimes that has to be even in spite of what they do!

Reflection number 134

FACING THE TRUTH

I think it was about 1904 when Brinsley McNamara wrote his classic novel, "Valley of the Squinting Windows"—its well worth a read. The author himself came from a very rural part of Ireland; his father had been a teacher in the local school. Unfortunately many of the villagers when they read his book recognised themselves as characters in his story. Locally this led to public outrage, while at the same time the rest of the country was thoroughly enjoying every page of his work. The book was burned in public. I'm told Brinsley's family had to leave town, and to this day his name still evokes strong reactions among many of the people who live there. What he wrote was actually too close to the bone. If he had weaved a story about people from another town, he would most likely have been hailed at home as the local literary hero. You could say that the people, in a very symbolic way, took him outside their village and threw him over the edge of a cliff, just like the locals tried to do with Jesus in the Gospel, when He told them the truth about themselves.

Truth is something that we don't always like hearing. We imagine that the truth is for someone else, but not for us. We love a good sermon in Church where the people sitting beside us end up with roaring red faces, but not us. How many of us are like the people in the Gospel, under an illusion that all our eggs are double yoked, that all our geese are swans and that we're whiter even than white itself? And sadly, whenever we're faced with the cold truth, we choose to ignore it, deny it, or become highly inflammable and kill the messenger.

One Sunday morning a priest began his homily by holding up a huge triangle. He then said, 'My homily this morning is like this triangle. It has three points.

The first point is this: Because we fail to listen, to accept, to love and to forgive each other as Jesus taught us, the people around us at home, at work, and in our community are hurting deeply.

The second point is: Most people really don't give a damn about this. The third point is: Most of you listening to me now are more concerned that I have used the word "damn", than you are about all the people who are hurting deeply.

The truth for some of us, is that very often we are not living and loving as Christ commands us to. How we choose to react to this, is entirely up to ourselves!

Reflection number 135

DON'T SWEAT THE SMALL STUFF

A few basic guidelines about living life to the full.

Remember, there is no way you can look as bad as that person on your driver's license.

Throw out non-essential numbers. This includes age, weight and height. Let the doctors worry about them, that's why you pay them.

Keep only cheerful friends. The grouches pull you down.

Keep learning. Learn more about computers, crafts, gardening, whatever. Never let your brain idle.

Enjoy the simple things. Laugh often, long and loud. Laugh until you gasp for breath.

Tears happen—it's all part of life, and nothing's ever going to change that. Endure, grieve, and keep trying every minute of every day to move on. Be "ALIVE" while you are alive.

Surround yourself with what you love, whether it's family, pets, keepsakes, music, plants, hobbies, whatever. Your home is your refuge.

Cherish your health: If it's good, preserve it. If it's unstable, improve it. If it's beyond what you can improve, get help, it's always available.

Don't take guilt trips. Take a trip to the shopping centre, to the next county, to a foreign country, but NOT to where the guilt is. Remember to be forgiving of yourself, as well as others.

Tell the people you love that you love them, at every opportunity.

Don't sweat the petty things and don't pet the sweaty things.

Hold on tight to the hand of Jesus—He's the only person who'll never leave you, and will always love you—not just because of what you do, but also in spite of what you do.

As we head into winter, by all means let's start saving for Christmas, let's lose those few inches from the waistline that we gained over the summer, but most important of all, lets commit to doing some real work on ourselves. Let's try to rid ourselves permanently of unhealthy baggage, let's try to build up our confidence and self-esteem, and instead of waiting for things to happen, let's make things happen. Let's try every day to believe in ourselves more, because when God made us, He made us in His image and in His likeness, and believe it or not, He definitely meant for us to be happy.

Reflection number 136

HOW OLD IS GRANDMA?

One evening, a grandson was talking to his grandmother about current affairs. The teenager asked his grandmother what she thought about shootings at schools, the computer age, and things in general.

His grandmother replied, "Well, let me think a minute, I was born before television, penicillin, polio shots, frozen foods, contact lenses and the pill. There was no radar, credit cards, laser beams, or ballpoint pens. Man had not invented air conditioners, dishwashers, clothes dryers, and the clothes were hung out to dry in the fresh air—no one had yet walked on the moon.

Your grandfather and I got married first and then lived together. Every family, I thought, had a father and a mother. Until I was 25, I called every man older than I, "Sir"—and after I turned 25, I still called policemen "Sir." We were before computer dating, dual careers, day care centres, and group therapy. The Ten Commandments, good judgment, and common sense governed our lives. We were taught to know the difference between right and wrong and to stand up and take responsibility for our actions. Serving your country was a privilege; living in this country was a bigger privilege.

We actually thought fast food was what people ate during Lent. Having a meaningful relationship meant getting along with your cousins. Draft dodgers were people who closed their front doors when the evening breeze started. Time-sharing meant time that a family spent together in the evenings and weekends, it was not purchasing apartments. We never heard of FM radios, CDs, DVDs, computers, yoghurt, or guys wearing earrings.

The term "making out" referred to how you did on your school exam. Pizza Hut, McDonald's, and instant coffee were unheard of. We had 5 & 10-cent stores where you could actually buy things for 5 and 10 cents.

Ice-cream cones, phone calls, spins on a streetcar, and a Pepsi were all a nickel. And if you did not want to splurge, you could spend your nickel on enough stamps to mail 1 letter and 2 postcards.

In my day, "grass" was mowed, "coke" was a cold drink, "pot" was something your mother cooked in, and "rock music" was your grandmother's lullaby. "Aids" were helpers in the Principal's office, "chip" meant a piece of wood, "hardware" was found in a hardware store, and "software" was not even a word.

No wonder people call us "old and confused" and say there is a generation gap . . . how old do you think I am?"

The grandmother was only 58 years old!

Reflection number 137

WAKE UP—IT'S ADVENT

Due to inherit a fortune when his sickly, widower father died, Charles decided he needed a woman with whom to enjoy it. Going into a singles' bar, he spotted a woman whose beauty immediately took his breath away.

"I'm just an ordinary man," he said, walking up to her, "but in just a week or two, my father will die, and I will inherit 20 million pounds." The woman happily went home with Charles that evening, and the very next day she became his stepmother.

Just another one of the many mistakes that men make . . . .

Very often we hear of stories just like the one written above, and we laugh. We think, how can people be so naive? How is it is possible to be so easily taken in? Surely it's only someone like the scarecrow in "The Wizard of Oz", a person with a head made of straw who would do such a thing, who would not stop to read the warning signs that are so obviously flashing all around. However, how many of us pride ourselves on being astute, intelligent, and of sound judgement, and yet we fail to read the warning signs that are given to us in scripture—we settle for so very little out of life, even though Jesus offers us so much more.

For many of us Advent is nothing more than a count down to Christmas—it lets us know how many days we have left to buy presents and get cards posted. We discovered all that when we learned how to make Blue Peter calendars. But that's not what Advent is about—Advent is a wake-up call, it's a challenge to leave the darkness in our lives behind, to set ourselves free, and to be a people of light.

Darkness takes on many forms for all of us—let's be honest about it, we are all human, we all have darkness. For some of us it can be a hatred that we hold on to, a lack of forgiveness or understanding for someone who has hurt us. For others it can be immoral behaviour or an addiction that controls us, but whatever our own personal darkness is, one thing's for sure, it's stopping us from being free, and from living our lives to the full.

Do you ever admit to yourself when you look around you on Christmas night, "I've achieved nothing here!" The new clothes, the expensive gifts, the rich food and elaborate parties often fail to make any difference in our lives—we're still the same old unhappy us, better dressed maybe, but still unhappy! Perhaps instead of making only cosmetic and monetary changes this Advent, we might try to make some internal changes that will start to change our lives around. One step at a time in the right direction is always a good beginning, and the right direction is walking towards the light.

Advent is about leaving our darkness behind. Let's heed the words of Isaiah this year where he says, "Come, let us walk in the light of the Lord!"

Reflection number 138

I DIDN'T SEE THAT ONE COMING

Little Paddy watched his Daddy's car pass by the school playground on a hot sunny afternoon and drive into the woods. As young boys are curious, he followed the car and saw his Daddy and none other than his aunt Jane clinched together in a passionate embrace in the back seat. Little Paddy found this all so funny that he laughed and laughed before running home to tell his mother. "Mammy, I was at the playground today and I saw daddy's car go into the woods behind the park with Aunt Jane sitting in the back seat. I ran to catch up with them, and there was daddy and Aunt Jane, clung together like new buckets, giving each other a big long kiss."

At this point the Mammy cut him off and said, "Paddy, this is such an interesting story, suppose you save the rest of it for supper time. I want to see the look on Daddy's face when you tell it tonight. Nanny and Granddad are joining us for supper and I have no doubt that they'll enjoy your funny story too." At the dinner table, Mammy invited little Paddy to tell everyone at the table what he saw happening that afternoon.

Paddy giggled and eventually started, "I was at the playground today and I saw daddy's car drive into the woods with Aunt Jane. When I caught up with them I saw that Daddy was giving Aunt Jane a big long kiss that lasted for about five minutes. It was all so funny because Aunt Jane and Daddy then started to do the exact same thing that mammy and Uncle Jimmy used to do when Daddy was away in the army."

The moral: Always listen to the whole story and don't ever interrupt.

Judging a person, trying to embarrass someone in company and passing comment on a neighbour or workmate is generally always a very bad idea. If you think you've no skeletons in your cupboard, remember that it's a long road that has no turn—we're all human, and because we're human, we're all prone to failing in one way or another, whether we care to admit that or not.

I've always found that the most compassionate people in the world are older people, people who've been there, people who've made the mistakes, learned the lessons and admitted their own humanity and frailty. There's something honourable about those who don't judge, not forgetting to mention Christian and wise—we have much to learn from them. Remember that when you point the finger at someone, be sure to look down at your own hand and notice that there are always three pointing back at you!

It hurts that, doesn't it?

Let's learn from Matthew 7:5 "Take the plank out of your own eye first, before you take the speck out of your brothers or sisters."

Reflection number 139

PEACE AND GOODWILL

One Sunday morning at Mass, a priest based his sermon around the Gospel theme, "Forgive Your Enemies". He talked about how human we all are, and about how difficult it can be at times to let go of hurts, grudges and resentment towards those who have wounded us. Coming towards the end of his homily, the priest casually asked his congregation (without ever expecting a response), "How many of us here have no enemies? How many of us are at peace with all those around us?" Suddenly out of the blue a small elderly lady who was sitting at the back of the Church raised her hand. "Mrs Jones," the priest said in a bewildered tone, "you are indeed a true Christian. What is your secret? How come you have no enemies?" Mrs Jones (who was aged about 97) stumbled down the aisle, faced the congregation, and laughed out loud: "To tell you truth Father, I've just outlived them all."

Loving those who have hurt us, used us, dropped us or wounded us can certainly be a painful one. It's indeed a job when their names come up in company not to actually spit feathers, hiss like a python or sit rigidly in the corner with a face on us like a busted guttie.

Part of the healing process for hurts and wounds can sometimes mean going to the person, or people who have injured us, confronting them openly, and letting them know just how much pain they have caused us to suffer. Very often it's vital for them to realize just what they have done to us, and what we believe to be unacceptable behaviour. Of course it goes without saying that it's also healthy for us to ventilate our anger properly—frozen anger is very often what makes depression.

If we're inclined to be nervous about confrontation, writing things down beforehand will make sure that we're well prepared and that we deliver our beliefs and feelings coherently, articulately and in apple pie order. Remember that God calls us all to forgive, to be free, to let go of hurts, but not to be used or walked over—silence in many cases is not golden, but instead is yellow.

When approaching Christmas we might try and make peace with all those whose names have over the years been struck off our Christmas card lists (for one reason or another). The Christmas message is one of peace and goodwill to all people—something which may take a lot of work, but it's definitely something which is well worth investing time and effort in!

Reflection number 140

WHAT GOES AROUND . . . .

One day a farmer's donkey fell down into a well. The animal cried piteously for hours as the farmer tried to figure out what to do. Finally, being the selfish old devil that he was, the farmer decided that as the animal was well past its best, and that the well needed to be covered up anyway; it just wasn't worth all the money and the effort that it would take to retrieve this old donkey. So, he invited some of his neighbours to come over and help him. They each grabbed a shovel and began to scoop dirt into the well. At first, the donkey realized what was happening and cried horribly, but then to everyone's bewilderment, after a few moments he quieted down. A few shovel loads later, the farmer looked down the well and was astonished at what he saw. With each shovel of dirt that hit the donkey's back he was doing something amazing. He was simply shaking the dirt off himself and stepping on top of it. As the farmer's neighbours continued to shovel dirt on top of him, he would shake it off and take a step up. Pretty soon everyone looked on as the donkey stepped up over the edge of the well and happily trotted off with his tail in the air.

The moral of the story: In reality life is going to shovel dirt on all of us—all kinds of dirt. The trick to getting out of the well is to shake the dirt off and take a step up. Each of our troubles is a stepping-stone; we can get out of our deepest troubles by never giving up.

Ps—Another ending to the story: *The same donkey later came back and bit the mean old farmer on the backside who had tried to bury him. The gash from the bite got infected, and the farmer eventually died in agony from septic shock. Remember, when you do something wrong, and try to cover your ass, it always comes back to bite you.* As my sister Dympna always says, "What goes around comes around!"

Reflection number 141

TAKING THE GOOD OUT OF EVERYTHING

Well, Christmas is over for another year. After New Year's Day trees and decorations will come down all around the city, and a day or so after the Feast of the Epiphany it's back to school and back to boring old routine once more.

Hope you enjoy this wee reflection: *Without wishing to be sexist or offensive in any way, what would have happened if Wise Women had visited Mary, Joseph and the Baby Jesus instead of three Wise Men? Well, being women they would have followed a map and asked directions from passers by instead of relying upon a star. Most likely they would have arrived on time, helped deliver the baby, brought practical gifts like babygros, nappies and sudocreme, cleaned the stable and then made a casserole.*

However, as they were leaving, they would most probably have whispered to each other, "Did you see the state of those sandals that Mary was wearing with that gown. I hear Joseph isn't even working. That donkey they travelled on has definitely seen better days. That baby doesn't look anything like Joseph. Mmmm, that drummer boy could beat his drum for me any time he liked. I wouldn't put money on it that we'll ever get the casserole dish back". And finally, "Miraculous birth my eye—I remember that Mary one at school—she was man mad!"

While it's only a joke, it reminds us of how guilty we all can be (*and can I stress that's both men and women*), of gossiping, taking away peoples characters and jumping to all the wrong conclusions. As we make our resolutions, one we might put at the top of our lists is not to judge, and if we're going to do a good turn for someone in need, don't tear the backside out of it as we leave!

Reflection number 142

WHAT LOVE IS . . .

Enjoy the story—it's another favourite of mine.

'It was a busy morning, approximately 8:30 am, when an elderly gentleman, in his 80's, arrived to have stitches removed from his thumb. He stated that he was in a hurry as he had an appointment at 9:00 am. I had him take a seat, knowing it would be over an hour before someone would to able to see him. I noticed that the man was looking at his watch a lot and I decided, since I was not busy with another patient, I would evaluate his wound. On examination it was well healed, so I talked to one of the doctors, got the needed supplies to remove his sutures and redress his wound. While taking care of his wound, we began to engage in conversation. I asked him if he had a doctor's appointment that morning, as he was in such a hurry. The gentleman told me no, that he needed to go to the nursing home to eat breakfast with his wife. I then enquired as to her health. He told me that she had been there for a while and that she was a victim of Alzheimer's disease. As we talked and I finished dressing his wound, I asked if she would be worried if he was a bit late. He replied that she no longer knew who he was, that she had not recognized him in five years now. I was surprised, and asked him. "And you still go every morning, even though she doesn't know who you are?" He smiled as he patted my hand and said, "She doesn't know me, but I still know who she is."

I had to hold back tears as he left, I had goose bumps on my arm, and thought, "That is the kind of love I want in my life." True love is neither physical, nor romantic. True love is an acceptance of all that is, has been, will be, and will not be.

It's worth noting that the happiest of people don't necessarily have the best of everything; they just make the best of everything that comes along their way!

Reflection number 143

FOOD GLORIOUS FOOD

T'was the month after Christmas, and all through the house
nothing would fit me, not even a blouse.
The cookies I'd nibbled, the eggnog I'd taste
at the holiday parties had gone to my waist.

When I got on the scales there arose such a number,
when I walked to the store (less a walk, more a lumber).
I'd remember the marvellous meals I'd prepared,
the gravies and sauces and beef nicely rared,
the cakes and the pies, the bread and the cheese
and the way I'd never said, "No thank you, please."

As I dressed myself in my husband's old shirt
And prepared once again to do battle with dirt
I said to myself, as I only can,
"You can't spend a winter disguised as a man!"
So, away with the last of the sour cream dip,
get rid of the fruit cake, every cracker and chip,
every last bit of food that I like must be banished,
'til all the additional ounces have vanished.
I won't have one cream bun, not even a lick.
I'll only chew on a long celery stick.
I won't have any biscuits, or corn bread, or pie,
I'll just munch on a carrot and quietly cry.
I'm hungry, I'm lonesome, and life is a bore . . .
But sure isn't that what January is for?
Unable to giggle, no longer a riot.
Happy New Year to all,
and to all a good diet!

As a student for the priesthood I have to admit that my greatest obsession was always food. I used to sit in the Theology Hall during lectures and dream about roast chickens and mouth-watering apple tarts. I can still remember the whiff of a fry that came from the priest's refectory each morning; while at the very same time we were subjected to a bowl of watery porridge. Those were the days when I could fully appreciate Christ's description of heaven as a banquet.

Times have definitely changed for me, and I strongly suspect for most of us here in Ireland too. We are now living in an age where over indulgence has become a way of life. Leaving aside the three regular meals that we are burdened with every day, our in-between meal consumption is enormous. When you count up the coffee break at 11.00am, the 4.00pm tea break, the light supper at bedtime, the odd bag of chips, the packet of crisps, the bar of chocolate and the glass of wine that we casually treat ourselves to; it all makes a staggering total. Should we be surprised that gluttony is listed as one of the seven deadly sins?

It might be good at this point to stop and ask ourselves: How much food and drink did we consume over the Christmas period? You don't have to tell anyone, but it's good just to count up the amount, even for yourself to see. The preachers of the world warn us solemnly—we are eating, drinking, smoking, and drugging ourselves to death.

Over the next few months our roads and pathways will play host to many of our citizens as they pound the poor innocent tar macadam in their designer psychedelic tracksuits. Well, any form of exercise is good—even if one of our main reasons is to be able to fit last years' clothes.

By all means let's fight the flab and get into shape for summer (it's very important for our health), but let's be sure to put as much energy and enthusiasm into saving our souls, as well as our bodies. On the last day, I really don't think Jesus is going to ask us; "How much do you weigh?"

Reflection number 144

SOMETIMES IT CAN BE HARD TO LOVE

A husband and wife were wakened one morning at around 3.00am by the sound of loud pounding on their front door. The husband struggled out of bed, made his way to the entrance of their home, and discovered a drunken man standing there in the pouring rain. Full of anger at being inconvenienced, he snarled at him, "Yes, what do you want?"

"Would you be so kind as to give me a push please?" the drunk man slurred. "Are you crazy?" the husband answered. "You've no chance!" "Have you no watch? Do you not realize that it's three o'clock in the morning?" and he slammed the door.

On returning to bed his wife asked, "Who was that at this unearthly hour?" "Oh, some drunk asking for a push," he mumbled, as he tried to get back to sleep. "Did you help him?" the wife asked. "No I didn't help him!" he exploded, "it's three in the morning, and it's raining cats and dogs out there!" "Well", she said, "You've got a very short memory". "Don't you remember the time when we were on our way to the party at your brother's house, and how those two young guys helped us fix a flat tyre? I'm very surprised at you. I was sure you would have helped that poor man in his hour of need!"

Wide-awake by this stage, and feeling somewhat guilty, the husband got up out of bed once more, dressed himself, and made his way to the front door. "Hey", he shouted. "Are you still out there?" "Yes," came the answer. "Do you still need a push?" he roared. "Yes," came the reply. Unable to see anything or anyone in the dark, he hollered, "Where are you?" The drunk man shouted back, "Over here . . . on the swing!"

If we want to be a source of light to those around us, the first thing we'll need is a warm heart, followed by a willingness to let it warm others who suffer from the cold—and that involves showing love during those times when we're confronted by situations where we want to pull our hair out. It means never being selective about who we care about, and never giving up on anyone.

In a world where so much value is placed on possessions, Jesus invites all of us to be apostles, and we can do this by simply caring for people in need.

Whenever we meet God on the last day, and we're all going to meet God on the last day, I imagine that his first question might be: "Now, explain to me how you showed love to all the people around you?"

What do you think you'll say in reply?

Reflection number 145

PARENTING

Let's face it, if raising children was going to be easy, it never would have started with something called **LABOUR**! After my sister Joan had her first child Mark, one of my cousins asked her had she "gone private" *(an expression used around Newry)* for the birth. After almost choking on her tea she replied angrily with copious amounts of steam coming out of her ears, "Go private! You must be joking! It was a painful enough experience without having to pay for it!"

Being a parent can certainly be a tough job—it's one where I feel compelled to genuflect and show the greatest respect and awe—hats off to parents all the way! A friend of mine recently described her feelings as being mentally, physically, emotionally and financially drained. Unfortunately, she was too tired to work out in which order they actually came. Her biggest nightmare is when one of her kids says to her, "Can I talk to you in private mum?" On one hand she's delighted that her children feel they can talk to her so openly, and on the other hand she's petrified as to what she is going to hear next.

It's very important to pray for parents in the challenging task of raising children today. They face a huge responsibility, and from what I can see, they definitely deserve commendation. As an outsider, parenting looks like a vocation of give, give, and more giving—for when children are hurt, parents hurt, and when children don't see the need to worry, their parents worry for them. Very often they don't like what their children do, but they never stop loving them, they never stop caring for them and they never stop hoping (very often against the odds) that things will get better—that sacred bond between parent and child is never really broken.

I enclose a heartfelt letter written by a father to his son who is growing through the turbulent teen years. It's a letter that's filled with such tremendous caring and understanding. Perhaps you might like to give it to your son or daughter some time when they're feeling hard done by or misunderstood. It goes like this . . . .

"I gave you life, but I cannot live it for you.
I can teach you things, but I cannot make you learn.
I can give you directions but I cannot be there to lead you.
I can allow you freedom, but I cannot account for you.
I can take you to Church, but I cannot make you believe.
I can teach you right from wrong, but I cannot always decide for you.
I can buy you beautiful clothes, but I cannot make you beautiful inside.
I can offer you advice, but I cannot accept it for you.
I can give you love, but I cannot force it upon you.
I can teach you to share, but I cannot make you unselfish.
I can teach you respect, but you must respect yourself first.
I can advise you about friends, but I cannot choose them for you.
I can advise you about sex, but I cannot make you pure.
I can tell you about the facts of life, but I can't build your reputation.
I can tell you about drink, but I can't say NO for you.
I can warn you about drugs, but I can't prevent you from using them
I can teach you about kindness, but I can't force you to be gracious.
I can warn you about sins, but I cannot make your morals.
I can love you as a child, but I cannot place you in God's family.
I can pray for you, but I cannot make you walk with God.
I can teach you about Jesus, but I cannot make Jesus your Lord.
I can teach you how to live, but I cannot give you eternal life!"

Reflection number 146

THE DANGER OF PUTTING THINGS OFF

George Phillips of Meridian, Mississippi was getting into bed one night when his wife told him that he'd left the light on in the garden shed, which she could see from their bedroom window. George went down the stairs and opened the back door to go turn off the light, when suddenly he became aware that there were people inside the shed stealing his belongings.

George immediately went back upstairs and phoned the police, who asked, "Is someone inside your house?" "No", replied George. "Well", they said, "unfortunately all our patrols are busy at the moment. Simply lock your front door and an officer will be along when available".

George hung up the telephone, counted to 30, and phoned the police a second time. "Hello", he said. "I just called you a few seconds ago because there were people in my shed. Just to let you know that you don't have to worry about them any more, because I've just shot them all". George then put the phone down.

Within minutes three police cars, an Armed Response unit, and an ambulance showed up at the Phillips' residence. Naturally, the police caught the burglars red-handed.

One of the policemen questioned George saying to him, "I thought you said that you'd shot the burglars?"

"Oh, not to worry" replied George. "It's so easy to get messages mixed up. Sure I thought you said there was nobody available!"

Going to the help of a neighbour, making the extra effort for someone in need, or as the gospel puts it, being the "Good Samaritan" can often be a difficult one. It's much easier just to think only of ourselves, to let everyone else fend for themselves, and adopt a "Mé Féin" attitude.

Trōcaire has a beautiful motto which simply says, "Lent is what you do!" It's my belief that on the last day God will ask us, "What did we do for those around us?" Let's hope we have plenty of examples to talk about!

Reflection number 147

KIDS TELL IT LIKE IT IS

The Gospel tells us that unless we become like little children we will never enter the kingdom of heaven. I suppose that means that we have to have the wonderful simplicity that children have, the innocent ways in which they always look at things, and the ways in which they can always hit the nail on the head, just when we're least expecting it. Enjoy the following illustrations of their strange and beautiful wit. A line from scripture springs out to me as I pen these examples—"Above the heaven is your majesty chanted by the mouths of children, babes in arm." Psalm 8:2. Enjoy!

A little girl was talking to her teacher one day about whales. The teacher said it was physically impossible for a whale to swallow a human being, because even though it was a very large mammal, its throat was very small. The child stated that in the Bible a whale swallowed the prophet Jonah. Irritated, the teacher reiterated that a whale could not swallow a whole human; it was physically impossible. The little girl shook her head and said, "I'm afraid I don't believe what you are saying. When I get to heaven I will ask Jonah." The teacher asked, "What if Jonah went to hell?" The little girl replied, "Well then, you ask him".

A Kindergarten teacher was observing her classroom of children while they were drawing. She would occasionally walk around to see each child's work. As she got to one little girl who was working diligently, she asked what the drawing was. The child replied, "I'm drawing God." The teacher paused and said, "But no one knows what God looks like." Without missing a beat, or looking up from her drawing, the girl replied, "Well, they will in a minute, when they see my picture."

The children in class seven had all been photographed, and the teacher was trying to persuade them each to buy a copy of the group picture. "Just think how nice it will be to look at this and smile when you are all grown up. You will be able to say, 'There's Jennifer, she's a lawyer,' or 'that's Michael, he's a doctor.' A small voice at the back of the room whispered," And there's the teacher, she's dead!"

Many children were lined up in the cafeteria of a Catholic Elementary School for lunch. At the head of the table was a large pile of apples. The Nun in charge wrote a note, and stuck it to the apple tray. It read: "Take only one. God is watching." Moving further along the lunch line, at the other end of the table was a large pile of chocolate chip cookies. One of the boys there nudged his friend and said, "Take all you want, God's watching the apples".

Reflection number 148

OPEN MY EYES LORD

A few prayers during Lent—"*Heavenly Father, help me remember that the woman who cut out in front of me in the traffic last night is a single mother—she worked nine hours that day, and is rushing home to cook dinner, help with homework, do the laundry and spend a few precious moments with her children.*

Help me to remember that the pierced, tattooed, disinterested young man who can't make up his mind what to order in the chip shop is a worried 19year-old college student, balancing his apprehension over final exams with a huge fear of not getting a student loan for the next term.

Remind us Lord that the scary looking man begging for money in the same spot every day (who in my opinion really ought to get a job!) is a slave to addictions that we can only imagine in our worst nightmares.

Help us to remember that the old couple who walk slowly up and down the supermarket aisle every morning and block our shopping progress are savouring their every moment. Based on the biopsy report she got back from the hospital last week, this may well be the last year that they go shopping together.

Heavenly Father, remind us each day that of all the gifts you give us, the greatest gift is love. It is not enough to share that love with those we hold dear. Open our hearts not just to those who are close to us, but to all humanity. Let us be slow to judge and quick to forgive; show patience, empathy and love.

Reflection number 149

HAVING MUM OVER FOR DINNER

God rest Rosemary Nelson, she was probably the most intelligent person, not to mention the most capable person that I have ever met. However, she always said that as much as she knew, she could never ever know as much as her mother. Was it that her mother had more education, more experience of life, or was it just that her mother brought her into the world, and for that reason alone she would always know what her daughter was thinking, feeling and experiencing? When you look at it like from that angle, perhaps that's why you can never pull the wool over your mother's eyes, and why mothers nearly always seem to be one step ahead of their children. Enjoy the story:—

Brian Hester invited his mother over for dinner. During the course of the meal, Brian's mother couldn't help but keep noticing how beautiful Brian's flatmate Stephanie was. Mrs. Hester had long been suspicious of a relationship between Brian and Stephanie, and over the course of the evening, while watching the two of them react, Mrs. Hester started to wonder if there was more between this "flat sharing" than met the eye. Reading his mother's thoughts, Brian quickly volunteered, "I know what you must be thinking Mum, but I assure you Stephanie and I are just flat mates."

About a week later, Stephanie came to Brian saying, "Ever since your mother was here for dinner, I've been unable to find the beautiful silver gravy ladle. You don't suppose she took it, do you?" Brian laughed and said, "Well, I could almost put my life on it that she didn't, but I'll drop her a line just to make sure." The following afternoon he sat down and wrote: Dear Mum: I'm not saying that you "did" take the gravy ladle from the house, and I'm not saying that you "did not" take the gravy ladle. But the fact remains that one has been missing ever since you were here for dinner. Can you shed any light on this matter? Love, Brian

Several days later, Brian received a letter from his mother that read: Dear Son: I'm not saying that you "do" sleep with Stephanie, and I'm not saying that you "do not" sleep with Stephanie. But the fact remains that if Stephanie was sleeping in her own bed, she would have found the gravy ladle by now. Love, Mum.

LESSON OF THE DAY . . . NEVER LIE TO YOUR MOTHER!

Reflection number 150

TOLL FREE CALLS

Mike from Kansas decided to write a book about church buildings around our world. He began his investigations by flying to San Francisco, and from there he started working his way east. Going into a very large Cathedral near "Frisco Bay" he began taking photographs and making copious notes. After a few moments Mike's eyes were drawn to a most beautiful golden telephone with a sign above it that read, "Calls $10,000 a minute." Seeking out the priest he asked him to clarify for him the meaning of golden telephone and its sign.

The priest explained that it was in fact a direct line to heaven, and if he paid the money required to make a call he could talk to God. Mike thanked the priest for this amazing information and continued on his way. As he visited churches in Seattle, Virginia, Michigan, Chicago, Milwaukee, and indeed around many parts of the world he found more golden telephones with the same sign.

Finally Mike arrived in Ireland. Upon entering a local church in the west he once again saw a golden telephone pinned to a wall, but strangely this time the sign above it read, "Calls 35 cents". Fascinated by the difference, he immediately went in search of the local priest. "Father," he said, "I have been to cities all over the world, and in many of the churches I have found the same golden telephone with a direct line to Heaven. I have been told that I could talk to God on this telephone, but in all the other churches the cost was $10,000 a minute. Your sign simply reads '35 cents a call'. Why is this?"

The priest smiling benignly at Mike, and replied, "Ach son, don't you realise you're in Ireland? Sure isn't that only the cost of a local call here!"

Talking to God is so simple and yet so precious. Why not give it a try? If you're not sure how to go about it, if you feel silly having a conversation with someone that you can't see, if you haven't prayed since you were a child at school, then why not begin by trying the wee prayer below—it's short, but it's very powerful. I bet there's something in the words that relate to you. Remember that prayer is what gives our life its direction and our problems their perspective. Enjoy!

Everyday I need thee Lord, but this day especially. I need some extra strength to face whatever is to be. This day more than any day I need to feel thee near, to build up my courage and to overcome my fears. By myself I just cannot meet the challenge of this hour—there are times when human creatures need a higher power, to help them bear what must be borne. And so dear Lord I pray, hold on to my trembling hands and please be with me today.

Reflection number 151

A LABOUR OF LOVE

Bet this reflection brings a tear to your eye.

Sitting at lunch one day my daughter casually mentioned that she and her husband were thinking of "starting a family." "We're taking a survey," she said half-joking. "What do you think?" "Well, it'll certainly change your life," I answered, carefully keeping my tone neutral. "Oh I know," she laughed, "no more sleeping in at the weekend, no more spur-of-the moment holidays away". But that's really not what I meant at all. I looked at my daughter, trying to decide what I should tell her. I wanted her to know what she will never ever learn in any books or childbirth classes.

I wanted to tell her that the physical wounds of child bearing will heal, but becoming a mother will leave her with an emotional wound so raw that she will forever be vulnerable. I considered warning her that she will never again read a newspaper without asking, "What if that had been my child?" That every plane crash and every house fire will haunt her. That when she sees pictures of starving children, she will wonder if anything could be worse than watching your child die.

I looked at her carefully manicured nails and her stylish suit and thought that no matter how sophisticated she was, becoming a mother would reduce her to the primitive level of a bear protecting her cub. That one urgent call of "Mammy!" will cause her to drop her best crystal without a single hesitation.

I felt that I should warn her that no matter how many years she has invested in her career, she will be professionally derailed by motherhood. She might arrange for childcare, but one day she will be going into an important business meeting and she will think of her baby's sweet smell. She will have to use every ounce of discipline to keep from running home, just to make sure her baby is all right.

I wanted my daughter to know that from now on every day decisions will no longer be routine. That a five year old boy's desire to go to the men's room rather than the women's at McDonald's will become a major dilemma. That right there, in the midst of clattering trays and screaming children, issues of independence and gender identity will be weighed against the prospect that a child molester might just be lurking in that restroom.

Looking at my beautiful daughter, I wanted to assure her that eventually she will shed the pounds of pregnancy, but she will never feel the same about herself. That her life, now so important, will be of less value to her once she has a child. That she would give herself up in a moment to save her offspring, but will also begin to hope for more years, not to accomplish her own dreams, but to watch her child accomplish theirs.

I wanted her to know that a caesarean scar or shiny stretch marks will become badges of honour. My daughter's relationship with her husband will change, and not in the way she thinks. I wished she could understand how much more you can love a man who knows how to powder the baby, or who never hesitates to play with his child. I think she should know that she will fall in love with him again for reasons she would now find very unromantic.

I wanted to describe to my daughter the exhilaration of seeing your child learn to ride a bike. I wanted to capture for her the belly laugh of a baby who is touching the soft fur of a dog or cat for the first time. I wanted her to taste the joy that is so real it actually hurts.

My daughter's quizzical look made me realise that tears had formed in my eyes. "You'll never regret it," I finally said. Then I reached across the table, squeezed my daughter's hand and offered a silent prayer for her, and for me, and for all the mere mortal women who stumble their way into this most wonderful of callings.

Reflection number 152

THREE THINGS

Hope you enjoy the following reflection and prayer—it's a favourite of mine, undeniably written by someone old and wise.

Three things in life that once gone, never come back—"Time Words, and Opportunity."

Three things in life that can never be lost—"Peace, Hope and Honesty."

Three things in life that are most valuable—"Love, Self-confidence and Friends."

Three things in life that are never always certain—"Dreams, Success and Money."

Three things that make a person—"Hard work, Sincerity and Commitment."

Three things in life that can destroy a person—"Addiction, Pride and Anger."

Three things that are truly constant—"Father, Son and Holy Spirit."

I ask the Lord to bless you, as I pray for you today; to guide you and protect you, as you go along your way. His love is always with you, His promises are true, and when you give Him all your cares, you know He'll see you through!

Reflection number 153

SET YOUR PRIORITIES

Enjoy the following modern day parable:

When things in your life seem almost too much to handle, when you're ready to pull your hair out with stress, when 24 hours in a day are not enough to get everything done, remember the story of the mayonnaise jar and the tea.

A teacher stood before a class of adolescent pupils and pointed to various items sitting on her desk. As they watched, the teacher picked up a large empty jar and proceeded to fill it up to the top with golf balls. She then asked the pupils if the jar was full. They agreed that it was. Next the teacher picked up a box of pebbles and poured them also into the jar. She then shook the jar lightly. The pebbles rolled into the open areas that were between the golf balls. Once again the teacher asked her pupils if the jar was full. They agreed that it was. After that she picked up a box of fine white sand that had been gathered at the seaside and she poured all of it into the same jar. Naturally the sand crept into every little nook and cranny. Once more she asked if the jar was full. The students responded this time with a unanimous "yes!" Finally the teacher produced two cups of tea from under her desk and poured the entire contents into the glass jar. The sand immediately soaked up the tea.

"Now," said the teacher, as the laughter subsided, "I want you to recognise that this jar represents your life. The golf balls are the important things—family, loved ones, health, friends, and faith in God—things that if everything else was lost and only these remained, our lives would still be very full indeed. The pebbles are the other things that matter, although not quite as important, things like jobs, houses, and cars. The sand represents everything else—the small things, the petty stuff—things like worrying about how we look, how much we weigh, trying to keep up with the Jones',

wondering what the neighbours will think and using time and energy arguing and fighting about things that are unimportant."

"Note that if we put the sand into the jar first," she continued, "there is no room for the pebbles or the golf balls. The same goes for life. If we spend all of our time and energy on the small things, the petty stuff, we will never have room for the things that are truly important to us. Pay attention to the things that are the keys to our happiness. Play with your children. Take time to get medical checkups. Take your family out to dinner. Go on holidays. Tell people you love them, again and again and again. Don't sweat the small stuff—remember that there will always be time to clean the house and fix the car. Take care of the golf balls first, the things that really matter. Set your priorities. The rest of course is just sand."

One of the pupils sitting in classroom raised his hand and enquired what the tea represented. The teacher smiled. "I'm glad you asked that," she said. "It just goes to show you that no matter how full your life may seem to be, there's always time to stop and have a cup of tea with a friend."

Reflection number 154

STRAIGHT TALK

In America, Bill Gates recently gave a speech at a High School about 11 things he felt young people did not and will not learn in school.

In his speech he talked about how feel-good and politically correct teachings created a generation of kids with no concept of reality and how this concept set them up for failure in the real world. The following are his personal guidelines for life.

1: *Life is not fair—get used to it.*

2: *The world won't care about your self-esteem. The world will expect you to accomplish something before you feel good about yourself.*

3: *You will not make £60,000 a year right out of High School. You won't be a vice-president of a company with a car phone until you earn both of them.*

4: *If you think your teacher is tough, wait 'til you get a boss.*

5: *Flipping burgers is not beneath your dignity. Your grandparents had a different word for burger flipping—they called it opportunity.*

6: *If you mess up, it's not your parents' fault. Don't whine on about mistakes, learn from them.*

7: *Before you were born, your parents weren't as boring as they are now. They got that way from paying your bills, cleaning your clothes and listening to you talk about how cool you think you* are. *So before you save the rain forest from the parasites of your parent's generation, try cleaning up the mess in your own bedroom first.*

8: *Your school may have done away with winners and losers, but life has not. In some schools they have abolished failing grades and they'll give you as many times as you want to get the right answer. This doesn't bear the slightest resemblance to anything in real life.*

9: *Life is not divided into semesters. You don't get summers off and very few employers are interested in helping you find yourself. Do that on your own time.*

10: *Television is not real life. In real life people actually have to leave the coffee shop and go to jobs.*

11: *Be nice to nerds. Chances are you'll end up working for one.*

If I could add a guideline myself, it would be from Max Ehrmann's Desiderata: "*Be at peace with God, whatever you conceive Him to be, and whatever your labours and aspirations in the noisy confusion of life, keep peace with your soul.*"

Reflection number 155

CRACKPOTS

This story is dedicated to me and all my wonderful crackpot friends.

An elderly Chinese woman had two large earthenware pots, each of them hung at the end of a pole which she carried across her shoulders.

The first pot had a small crack in it, while the second did not and always delivered a full portion of water. At the end of the long walk from the stream to the old woman's home, the cracked pot arrived only half full.

For many years she travelled back and forward to the stream on a daily basis, always bringing back only one and a half pots of water. Naturally enough the perfect pot was proud of its accomplishments, but sadly the poor cracked pot was ashamed of what it saw as its' imperfection, and was miserable that it could only do half of what it had been made to do.

After a long time of what it perceived to be bitter failure, the earthenware pot spoke to the old woman as it sat one day by the side of the stream. "I am ashamed of myself ", it said, "this crack, this imperfection in my side causes me to leak water all the way back to your home."

The old woman smiled serenely, "Did you notice that there are flowers on your side of the path, but not on the other pot's side? Well, that's because I have always known about this little flaw, as you call it, so I planted flower seeds on your side of the path, and every day while we journey back to our home, you water them. For years now I have been able to pick all these beautiful flowers to decorate my table. Without you being just the way you are, there would not be this beauty to grace our home."

Each of us has what we sometimes see as our own unique wonderful flaw. Remember that it's the cracks, the flaws and dare I say the "imperfections" that make our lives all the more human and indeed rewarding. Let's work hard each day at trying to accept and love the people all around us exactly the way God has made them.

Each one of us is in the mind of God for all eternity—He has a plan for every single individual, never forget we are all made in His image and His likeness.

"Before I formed you in the womb I knew you; before you came to birth I consecrated you; I have appointed you as a prophet to the nations." Jeremiah 1:5

Reflection number 156

LOVE YOURSELF

I adore this particular piece of scripture. It's taken from St. Paul's letter to the Corinthians 12:31-13:8

"Be ambitious for the higher gifts. And I am going to show you a way that is better than any of them.

If I have the eloquence of all people or of angels, but am without love, I am simply a gong booming or a cymbal clashing. If I have the gift of prophecy, understanding all the mysteries there are, and knowing everything, and if I have faith in all its fullness to move mountains, but without love, then I am nothing at all. If I give away all that I possess, piece by piece, and if I even let them take my body to burn it, but am without love, it will do me no good whatever.

Love is always patient and kind; it is never jealous; love is never boastful or conceited; it is never rude or selfish; it does not take offence, and is not resentful. Love takes no pleasure in other people's sins but delights in the truth; it is always ready to excuse, to trust, to hope, and to endure whatever comes.

Love does not come to an end".

Remember in life there will always be someone better looking than you—that's just the way life is. There will always be someone smarter, someone with a bigger and fancier house, who drives a more expensive and much faster car. It goes without saying that their children will naturally do better in school, and their spouse will be a much better cook or be able to fix more things around the house—we've all met those type of people, they're everywhere, and good luck to them. So why not let it all go, and just love yourself and your own circumstances. What we need around us is complementation, not competition.

Think about it, the most beautiful person in the world can also have hell in their heart, and the most highly favoured person at your workplace may be unable to have children. And as for the richest person that you know, they may have the car, the house, the holidays and the clothes, but they may also be crucified with loneliness or personal disappointment. The Word of God says, "If I have not Love, I am nothing at all."

So, love yourself. Love who you are—you're made in the image and the likeness of God. Look in the mirror first thing in the morning, smile back at yourself and say "I am too blessed to be stressed and much too anointed to be disappointed!" Remember, winners make things happen and losers let things happen—it's all up to you. Life's all about choices—you choose how you want it to be. To the world you might just be one person, but to one person you just might be the world!

Reflection number 157

TELL THE TRUTH AND SHAME THE DEVIL

One day, as a seamstress was sewing, her thimble fell into the river nearby. When she cried out, the Lord appeared to her and asked, "My child, what's wrong?" The seamstress replied that her thimble had fallen into the water and that she needed it to help make a living for her and her family. The Lord gently dipped His hand into the water and pulled up a golden thimble that was set with pearls. "Is this your thimble?" He asked. The seamstress looked at it and replied, "No." The Lord again dipped his hand into the river, this time He held before her a silver thimble that was ringed with sapphires. "Is this your thimble?" the Lord asked. Again, the seamstress replied, "No." The Lord reached down again and finally came up with an old worn out leather thimble. "Is this your thimble?" the Lord asked. The seamstress smiled and replied, "Yes, oh yes Lord. Thank you so much." The Lord was pleased with the old woman's honesty and gave her all three thimbles to keep. The seamstress went home very happy.

Some years later the seamstress was walking along the same riverbank when the husband who had been walking beside her accidentally fell into the water and disappeared. When the woman cried out, the Lord again appeared and asked, "My dear, why are you crying?" "Oh Lord," she said "my poor old husband has fallen into the river! Please, please help me!" The Lord reached down into the dark water and came up with a very wet but ruggedly handsome Mel Gibson. "Is this your husband?" the Lord asked. "Yes Lord, oh yes, absolutely he is!" cried the seamstress, "I'd recognize my man anywhere!" The Lord was furious. "You lied! How could you do such a terrible thing?" The old seamstress hung her head in shame and said, "Oh forgive me Lord. Forgive me please. It is a simple misunderstanding that any woman could make. You see; if I had said 'no' to Mel Gibson, you would have probably come up with Tom Cruise. And if I said 'no' to him, no doubt you would have finally come up with my husband. Had I then said 'yes,' you would have then given me all three men to take home. Lord, I'm not in the best of health and at my stage in life would not be fit to take care of all three, so that's why I said 'yes' to Mel Gibson. Besides I'm a Christian woman, and the truth is I really want to get poor Mel out of those soaking wet clothes before he catches his death of cold. It's Mel's best interest that I have at heart. What's more I have a big log fire at home that he could warm himself in front of."

The moral of this story is: Whenever a woman spins a story, it's for a good and honourable reason, and always in the best interest of others.

While telling yarns is very funny, telling lies is not—lies are not funny, they hurt and they do untold damage to innocent people. However hard we dress up our falsehoods, fabricated stories, fibs and misrepresentations, they are still untruths and they are always used with the intention to mislead.

"Tell the truth and shame the devil", was an expression that was drummed into me as a child. It's not a bad one to try and live by!

Reflection number 158

SPEAK WORDS OF LOVE NOT WAR

A young couple drove along a country road for several miles without exchanging a single word. An earlier discussion at home had led to a heated argument, and as you can imagine neither of them wanted to concede their position. As they passed by a field of goats the husband turned to his wife and asked sarcastically, "Relatives of yours?" "Yep," she replied, "in-laws!"

Sadly now it's often "open season" when a couple row or fall out. Debasement, degradation and verbal assassination sadly seem to have become today's ways of making your point. I suppose that type of communication can easily seem the norm for those who think that Jeremy Kyle or Trisha Goddard are the standards. I still believe (probably naively) that if someone truly loves you, surely they would never ever humiliate you like that. Sarcasm, cynicism and disparagement are like cancer—they do incalculable damage internally and cause inconceivable pain.

I enclose a few words from St. Paul to the people at Rome, Chapter 12. Personally it's an old favourite of mine, and one that many couples choose to have read at their wedding ceremony. It's certainly a good guide for all of us in our relationships.

"Do not let your love be a pretence, but sincerely prefer good to evil. Love each other as much as brothers and sisters should and have a deep respect for each other. Work for the Lord with untiring effort and with great earnestness of spirit. If you have hope, this will make you cheerful. Do not give up if trials come your way but keep on praying. If anyone is in need you must share with them, making hospitality your special concern. Bless those

who persecute you; never curse them, bless them. Rejoice with those who are happy and be sad with those who are in sorrow. Treat everyone with equal kindness and never be condescending. Do all you can to live at peace with those around you."

Reflection number 159

DEAR ME

A common sense reflection.

Dear ME,

I noticed with great concern this morning how tired and drawn looking you are. Your skin looks pale and dull, and your eyes lack that sparkle that was once so appealing. Those frown marks between your eyes are becoming more prominent—a constant reminder of the weight of the world you carry on your shoulders. You were up late again last night finishing work, and what with one of the children being sick during the night you didn't get any sleep. With a hectic day today as usual—school runs, dental appointments, cooking, cleaning, sick children, be back in time to collect the little ones from School—there appears to be no sign of any change for the better. Quite frankly ME, quality of life sucks around here. When was the last time you had time for ME—had a good laugh, did something just for ME? This cannot go on!

ME! You have got to start taking responsibility! You are not taking sufficient care of ME. You cannot survive this pace of life. Warning—you are on the slippery slope to self-destruction!

ME, you are the most important person in the world. If you don't look after ME, no one else will, and indeed the people whom you say you love will all suffer.

ME, you have got to start taking better care of yourself, the way you are treating ME is not Christian, in fact it is cruel. You are the most considerate, thoughtful, creative, imaginative, intelligent, humorous, generous and beautiful person I know. You have devoted your life to those around you, giving of your emotional, intellectual, physical and spiritual self. You are withering away because you are simply not on a path of renewal and growth. Your self-esteem is low and you are mentally, physically and emotionally exhausted. Constantly on overdrive you are suffering, and all around you your loved ones are suffering too. You need to start taking care of ME. Cherish ME, speak nicely to ME. Compliment ME. Give ME treats. Stop Worrying—it may never happen! Read ME a book. Feed ME with only healthy nutritious food. Enjoy more physical intimacy. Allow ME to speak my true feelings. Take ME to the cinema or theatre. Meditate, create time for ME to pray and talk to my God. Bring ME for a walk so that I can fill my lungs with fresh air, oxygenating the blood that gives me life. ME, you deserve to live; to have life to the full as Christ talked about, to have all your physical, emotional, intellectual and spiritual needs met! When are you going to start to do something about it?

Sincerely,
Your wake-up-call!

Reflection number 160

SEEING WHAT NO ONE ELSE CAN SEE

A farmer had some puppies that he needed to sell. He painted a sign advertising the four pups, and set about nailing it to a post on the edge of his yard. As he was driving the last nail into the post he felt a tug on his overalls. He looked down into the eyes of little boy.

"Mister", he said, "I want to buy one of your puppies".

"Well", said the farmer as he rubbed the sweat off his neck, "these puppies come from fine parents, they have all their official papers and they cost a great deal of money".

The boy dropped his head for a moment. Then reaching deep into his pocket he pulled out a handful of coins and held it up to the farmer.

"I've got 39 pence. Is that enough to take a look?"

"Sure", said the farmer, and with that he let out a whistle. "Here Dolly", he called. Suddenly, out from the doghouse and down the ramp ran Dolly followed by four little balls of fur.

The little boy pressed his face against the wire fence that looked into the pen. His eyes danced with delight. As the dogs made their way to the fence the little boy noticed something else stirring inside the doghouse. Slowly another little ball of fur appeared, this one noticeably smaller. Down the ramp it slid, and in a somewhat awkward manner the little pup began hobbling towards the others, doing its very best to catch up.

"I want that one", the little boy said, pointing to the runt.

The farmer knelt by the boy's side. "Son, you don't want that puppy", he said. "He'll never be able to run and play with you like the other dogs would".

The little boy stepped back from the fence and began rolling up one leg of his trousers. In doing so he revealed a steel brace running down both sides of his leg attaching itself to a specially made shoe.

Looking back at the farmer he said, "You see, I can't run too well myself, and surely that wee dog will need someone who understands him". With tears in his eyes the big farmer picked up the little pup. Holding it carefully he handed it to the boy.

"How much is he"? asked the boy. "Oh, no charge", answered the farmer. Sure there's never any charge for love".

When you think about it, our world is full of people, and all they need is someone who understands!

Reflection number 161

SHOULD OUR DIFFERENCES NOT UNITE US?

A young boy was walking home from Mass one Sunday morning when he arrived at a crossroads where he met a young girl coming from the other direction. "Hello," he said, beaming from ear to ear. "Hi," the girl replied.

"Where are you going?" he asked. "Well, I've just been to Church this morning and I'm now on my way home," she answered. "Me too," he replied. "Which Church do you go to?" "Why I go to the Baptist Church back down the road," replied the girl. "What about you?" "Oh I go to the Catholic Church back at the top of the hill," he said.

As they chatted the young couple discovered that they were both travelling in the same direction, so they walked along together exchanging stories and craic about school and friendship. After a few hundred yards they suddenly came to a low spot in the road where spring rains had partially flooded the ground, and it looked as if there was no way that they could possibly get across to the other side without getting wet.

"If I get my new Sunday dress wet my Mum's going to skin me alive," said the girl. "My Mum'll kill me too if I get my new Sunday suit wet," replied the boy. "She never stops giving out to me about keeping myself clean."

"I'll tell you what I'm gonna do," said the girl. "I'm gonna take off my dress, hold it up over my head and wade across the water". "That's a great idea," replied the boy. "I'm going to do the same thing with my suit." Without further ado they both undressed and waded their way across without getting any of their clothes wet. As they stood there in the sun, waiting to drip dry before putting their clothes back on the boy remarked in all innocence, "You know, I never did realise before how much of a difference there really is between a Baptist and a Catholic."

In life there are so many different groupings, so many different labels and different titles (often one foolishly considered better than the other). To name a few we have male/female, Catholic/Protestant, black/white, straight/gay, working class/middle class, Irish/British, and let's not forget the famous old chestnuts, rich and poor. Sadly we have become so used to making comparisons, looking for differences, putting people in pigeon holes and constantly compartmentalising that we lose sight of what is really important—PEOPLE! And what unites us all together is that we are all made in the image and likeness of God.

I wonder though how many people really believe that about themselves when they look in the mirror, and better still how many of us see God in the people around us every day? If we did, then surely savage terms such as racism, class distinction and homophobia would never need to exist!

Reflection number 162

SEPARATING THE WHEAT FROM THE CHAFF

What type of a person are you?

'An old man and his dog were walking along a road, enjoying the scenery, when it suddenly occurred to the old man that he was dead, and that the dog walking beside him had also been dead for years. The old man wondered where this road was leading them. After a while they came to a high white stone wall along one side of the road, broken by a tall arch that glowed in the sunlight. Standing before it the old man saw a magnificent gate in the arch that looked like Mother of Pearl—the street that led to the gate was made of pure gold.

Walking towards the gate the traveller saw a man with a beard sitting at a desk. When he was close enough, he called out, "Excuse me, where are we?"

"This is Heaven," the man with the beard answered. "Wow! Heaven! Amazing! Would you happen to have some water?" he asked. "Of course, sir. Come right on in, and I'll have some refreshing iced water brought up for you." The man gestured, and the gate began to open. "Can my friend," nodding toward his dog, "come in, too?" the traveller asked. "I'm sorry sir, but it is our policy that we don't accept pets here." The old man thought for a moment, turned back towards the road and continued on his way.

After another long walk, and at the top of another long hill, they came to a dirt track. As the old man and his tired dog approached a gate leading into a field he saw another man with a beard man inside, leaning against a tree and reading a book. "Excuse me!" he called to the reader. "Do you have any water?" "Yeah, sure, there's a pump over there. Come on in—you're welcome!" "How about my friend here?" the traveller said as he gestured to his dog. "There should be a bowl by the pump", the bearded man replied. They went through the gate, and sure enough, there was an old-fashioned hand pump with a bowl sitting beside it.

The traveller filled the bowl and took a long drink, then he gave some water to his dog. When they were full, he and the dog walked back towards the bearded man who was standing by the tree waiting for them. "What do you call this place?" the traveller asked. "This is Heaven," he answered as he bent down and patted the dog. "Well, that's confusing," the traveller said. "The man down the road said that was Heaven, too." "Oh, you mean the place with the pure gold street and the pearly gates? Nope. That's Hell."

"Doesn't it make you angry when they use your name like that?" "No, not at all! I can see how you might think that, but we're just happy that they weed out the ones who'll leave their best friends behind!'"

Reflection number 163

A MENTION OF OUR SAVIOUR

I couldn't believe it when I came across the following reflection that it would end up mentioning Jesus. It's funny and weird and also strangely true in many ways. Enjoy!

As I mature, I've learned that you cannot make someone love you. All you can do is stalk them and hope that they panic and give in.

I've learned that no matter how much I care for those around me and try to love my neighbour, some people are just assholes.

I've learned that it takes years to build up trust, and it only takes suspicion, not proof to knock it down.

I've learned that you should never compare yourself to others—they are usually much more screwed up than you are.

I've learned that we are responsible for what we do, unless we are celebrities.

I've learned that regardless of how wonderfully romantic a relationship is at first, the passion always fades and there had better be a lot of money to take its place.

I've learned that 99% of the time when something in your home isn't working, one of your kids did it.

I've learned that the people you care about most in life are taken away from you too soon, and all the less important ones never go away.

I've learned that if you don't know the Lord Jesus personally, you really are one sad and lonely individual.

Knowing the Lord personally truly is a beautiful gift. Without faith or belief in the Lord we are so pitifully poor!

Reflection number 164

I AM THANKFUL FOR . . . .

A wee reflection for us to mull over when we feel hard done by and in the mood for complaining.

Lord, I am thankful:

For the wife who says it's chips for tea tonight, because she is home with me and not out with someone else. For the husband who is on the sofa being a couch potato, because he is home with me and not out at the pub.

For the teenager who is complaining about doing dishes, because it means that he or she is at home, and not out on the streets.

For the taxes I pay, because it means I am employed.

For the mess I have to clean up after a party, because it means I have been surrounded all evening by my friends.

For the clothes that fit a little too snug, because it means I have more than enough to eat.

For my shadow that watches me work, because it means I am in the sunshine.

For a lawn that needs mowing, windows that need cleaning, and gutters that need fixing, because it means I have a home.

For all the complaining I hear about the local council and the government, because it means we have freedom of speech.

For the parking spot I find at the far end of the parking lot, because it means I am capable of walking and I have been blessed with transportation.

For my huge heating bill, because it means I am very warm.

For the lady behind me in Church who sings off key, because it means I can hear.

For the pile of laundry and ironing, because it means I have clothes to wear.

For weariness and aching muscles at the end of the day, because it means I am capable of working hard.

For the alarm that goes off in the early morning hours, because it truly means I am alive.

For unanswered prayers, because God always knows best, and the happiest person in the world is not the one who has the most, but the one who needs the least.

Reflection number 165

THE INTERVIEW WITH GOD

'I dreamed I had an interview with God. *"So you would like to interview me?"* God asked.

"If you have the time?" I said. *"My time is eternity. What questions do you have in mind for me?"*

"What surprises you most about humankind?"

God answered, *"That they get bored with childhood, they rush to grow up and then long to be children again.*

That they lose their health to make money and then lose their money to restore health.

That by thinking anxiously about the future they forget the present, such that they live in neither the present nor the future.

That they live as if they will never die, and die as though they had never lived."

God's hand took mine and we were silent for a while.

Then I asked, *"As a parent, what are some of life's lessons you want your children to learn?"*

"To learn that they cannot make anyone love them. All they can do is let themselves be loved.

To learn that it is not good to compare yourself to others.

To learnt to forgive by practicing forgiveness.

To learn that it only takes seconds to open profound wounds in those we love, and it can take many years to heal them.

To learn that a rich person is not one who has the most, but is one who needs the least.

To learn that there are people who love them dearly, but simply do not yet know how to express or show their feelings.

To learn that two people can look at the same thing and see it differently.

To learn that it is not enough that they forgive one another but that they must also forgive themselves."

"Thank you for your time," I said humbly.

"Is there anything else you'd like your children to know?"

*God smiled and said, "Just know that I am here for you, **ALWAYS!**"*